THE WORD WITHIN

Other books by Father Peter Bowes:

The Way, the Truth and the Life:
The Autobiography of a Christian Master

Steps on the Way

Spiritual Astrology

The Radical Path

Pearls of a Fisherman

Sayings of a Christian Master Teacher

Love is Simple

Sermons from the Valley

The Joy of Stretching

Father Peter Bowes

THE WORD WITHIN

Sophia Publishing

Woodstock, IL

The Word Within
By Father Peter Bowes

Sophia Publishing 2016

The Word Within
3rd Edition

ISBN 978-1-4116-9788-1

All citations of *Poem of the Man-God* provided with
permission from:
Centro Editoriale Valtortiano
I 03036 Isola del Liri (Fr) – Italia
Tel. +39 0776 807 032 – Fax +39 07776 809 789
www.mariavaltorta.com   cev@mariavaltorta.com

For information, write to:
Sophia Publishing
509 E. Kimball Ave. Woodstock, IL 60098

Cover Art: Meira Leonard

ACKNOWLEDGEMENTS

This book was made possible by the loving efforts and dedication of the following people:

Father Paul Blighton, whose teaching and courage provided me with the spiritual school that I so long awaited. His experience of God, passed on to me through those he taught, has changed my life, making me in many ways a better reflection of God than otherwise I would have been.

Robert Harrison, Master Marthelia McCaffrey, and Master Raeson Ruiz, whose training by Father Paul enabled them to faithfully train me and guide me to my experiences of the Light of Christ and Self-Realization.

CONTENTS

"The Kingdom of God is within you."
- Jesus Christ

ॐ

INTRODUCTION

There is an old story of a very wise Buddhist monk who was visited by a man seeking enlightenment. After waiting for a time, the man finally received an audience with the monk, who proceeded to serve his guest a cup of tea. The monk began to pour the tea into the man's cup. When it was full, the monk continued to pour, until it overflowed onto the saucer and onto the table, spilling onto the floor.

The man became very uncomfortable and complained to the monk. "Sir, you are spilling tea all over the floor; can't you see that my cup is full?" The monk smiled at him and said, "You are right; your cup is full. You are not ready for instruction."

The man went away very disappointed, and quite humiliated. The monk correctly perceived that the man was trying to squeeze enlightenment into a head already full of conceptions. So many times, we listen to others through the noise of our own crystallized opinions, leaving no room for a fresh look at things or for new experiences.

When I was baptized as a little baby, the priest told my parents, "This boy will be a priest." I remember wanting to be a priest for much of my elementary school years. My parents sent me and my siblings to Catholic private schools. For my parents, education, music lessons, and discipline were the most important things to pass on to the children. Each child had to play a musical instrument and go to the finest private schools.

As a young boy, I had an intense desire for truth. I felt there was something within me that was more real and essential than anything that I perceived in the physical world. Truth had to be something that did not change. I intuitively conceived truth to be an ultimate experience that I could count on. Many people feel truth is relative. I could not agree. Opinions, beliefs, and trends are relative. But I always wanted to know and believed there were abiding truths within the universe. I wanted to know what was beyond mere opinions, beliefs, and trends. I wanted to know things with such clarity that I could not doubt them, truths which were made so by the reality of my own experience.

I remember my first Holy Communion as an exhilarating, blessed day. The Communion host tasted so good that I sneaked back into the sacristy while others were celebrating, and I ate a whole stack of the quartershaped hosts. I was under the impression that, if some was good, more was better. Though I did feel a little guilty about it, I figured Jesus would want me to have as much of him as I could get. In my religion classes, I was the student who incessantly asked the question "Why?" driving my teachers to frustration. Even if the teachers were not able to answer my questions, I kept asking. Soon the universe answered me. My inquisitiveness was a blessing for me that opened the door to real answers, to an awakening of real truth in my life. The result of my seeking was that I found what I had sought, and now I am able to help others in their quest for the truth.

A short sixteen-and-a-half-year stay with my family of origin was a rather sour beginning to this life. My father was an army physician. He spent ten years as an obstetrician and assisted at the births of all his children. After that, he became an epidemiologist and ran health departments in various cities. His role as a disciplinarian was in making decisions about which particular corporal punishments were to be administered to the children. (Since he was so busy working to support our enormous family, my mother was the one left with the day-to-day administering of the regular doses of discipline.) My father was an old-school patriarch who needed to be more important than everyone else. As a military man, he applied military discipline to his children, imposing dress code, manners, and everyone needing to take their assigned seats at the table.

Usually a quick scan of the room gave any observer an instant awareness of the children's chronological ages, youngest to oldest, as usually they were sitting in order of their arrival on the planet. Before I reached age twelve, it would have been unthinkable to question these standards and methods. Repercussions for insubordination included criticism, ridicule, cynicism and various forms of corporal punishment. Dissent was a risk only few of the children would take. Eventually, in my family, I became notorious for taking that avenue.

I remember my first spanking at four years old, with a maple "Fuller Brush" clothes brush. Brushes like that were well-made of fine hardwood. I had walked down the street unsupervised, following after a horse-drawn carriage into which the workers pitched the leaves from the curb. The horses were so beautiful and inspiring, the fall leaves smelling so fresh, and the sun shining so brightly that I was taken up in the pageantry and followed around the block as they worked. Apparently, my mother had anticipated my absence and walked around the block the other way to retrieve me. Meanwhile, I had backtracked three-quarters of the way around and came home. When I got home, she was furious with me, and she broke that maple brush over my rear end. That was my first violent disciplinary experience. The clouds seemed to come crashing in after that episode, and I realized I was not in heaven anymore. I was definitely on earth, and it was not much fun.

School Days 57-58

School Days 59-60

4

My mother was a homemaker who, after bearing thirteen children, went back to school for her doctorate in Theology. Her emphases were Old Testament Prophets and Greek and Hebrew linguistics. Both of my parents were only children who had alcoholic fathers and were raised by single moms and the nuns who educated them. My dad married my mother for her intelligence and good genes. Neither indulged in alcohol, cigarettes, or coffee. The family values set to be impressed upon us centered around education and music, both of which were administered stressfully and without joy.

My siblings and I calculated that my mother was pregnant for a total of ten and a half years. Every year and a half, another sibling was born. In eighteen years, thirteen children were born. No twins. I was the fourth child and second male. Growing up, my experience was being alone in a crowd. The only time the family acted as a unit was when we were in some athletic contest with neighbor children and felt compelled at least to look like we were of one mind and one body. That certainly was not the way things went inside our home.

I recall a particularly difficult discussion with my mother when I was twelve. It was summer, and I did not want to go to church anymore. I said, "I don't get anything out of going to church, so I'm not going anymore." She said, "You can't stop going and that's that." I said, "I'm not going." She said, "Yes, you are," and I said, "No, I'm not." This interchange went back and forth many times, until she was frustrated with me and went to retrieve one of the many barn wood sticks about 18 inches long off one of the bureaus or mantles in the house. She was going to discipline me for insolence and arguing and came at me with the "board of education."

As she approached, I grabbed it out of her hand and broke it over my knee, saying, "Don't ever touch me again." She was quite shocked. Then I went upstairs, packed my bag, and proceeded to walk out the front door as she was screaming for me to come back. I walked across the street and began hitchhiking to Connecticut, to live with my 16-year-old girlfriend. (Our all-boys school had dances with various girls' schools in New England, and I had met a nice girl with whom I had been corresponding.) I stayed with her for ten days, then hitchhiked home, and nothing was said about it. I took this silence as tacit permission to visit my brother in New York as often as I liked for the next few years.

The most blissful and enjoyable time in my early life was being in nature outside my home. Running through the woods was exciting and enjoyable, as was sailing our sailboat on the Narragansett Bay in Rhode Island, or making houses out of driftwood on the beach. My life away from home was alive with adventure, while my home life was stifling, dead, and scary. I learned about God by observing nature, feeling the weather change, seeing the organized pattern of creation as it played out in the beauty and wonder of existence. I was in awe. I felt so full of amazement that a world so beautiful existed for everyone to experience.

Truly, my personal world away from home was in stark contrast with everyday home life. I had difficulty imagining what life would be like if I had conscious parents and a peaceful home. I later decided it is more practical to believe that some people come into earth-life parentless, which gives them the advantage of being able to look to a much higher source for true parenting. In a way, I see my childhood as a mixed blessing, where I learned to appreciate being guided by life and led by experiences, rather than by my caregivers. In fact, all twelve of my siblings learned to be incredibly independent, each carving out a slice of undisturbed space in an already crowded life.

Age 13 in Rhode Island

Age 14 in Rhode Island

At twelve, I got my first job in a lobster restaurant, as a dishwasher. I enjoyed the money immensely, as I did not have to wear the hand-me-downs from my older brother anymore. I was able to purchase my own shoes, boots, and jeans. Then I met a potato and nursery farmer on Newport Island that needed workers, so I hired on as a laborer doing whatever he needed. This turned out to be my summer job for the next few summers. Now I could make my clothes and entertainment money without need of any help from my parents. Our family was not poor, but it was so regimented that no entertainment or choice in clothes was possible. Occasionally a symphony or religious event was a compulsory outing for everyone.

During my fourteenth year, my parents anticipated a job change for my father to Indianapolis. To prevent any disruptions in our schooling, they sent me and my older sister to Indianapolis to live with a family until they were going to move in October that fall. That move did not happen as planned, and so we stayed with two families my entire sophomore year. I was so independent and capable of getting around the new city that it was very stifling being back with my parents when they finally moved and got a big house in Indianapolis. I spent my 10th grade year at a Catholic, all-boys school and was experimenting with drugs with my friends. I did manage to be on the wrestling team that year and was city-champ in my weight class. During junior year, I was miserable at home, since the parents had moved and I was living with them again. I had met a few friends and began demanding that I go to public school. Finally, my parents relented and let me go.

When I was sixteen, I moved in with my high school French teacher, who had noticed my academic abilities, even though my under-achieving status caused him some concern. My best friend and I moved into his house, since we were the most promising of his students and he wanted to work with us more closely. Also, we both had some serious difficulties living with our parents. I was younger than most students in my class at school. I had skipped fourth grade, because I admired my third grade teacher, Sister Cecilia, so much I would have learned calculus for her. She had given me as much work in third grade as I could accomplish, and I had quickly gone through all the third grade material. Her love and support had been so unusual and inviting for me. She was an extreme contrast to my family life. Mathematics was not easy for me, but my admiration for her had forced me to overcome those limitations. None of the teachers until the middle of high school had been as influential as she was. The years at home had dampened my spirit to such an extent that my grades and performance in school had suffered proportionately.

After a tumultuous first half of my senior year, I enrolled in Indiana University. That was a week after I had turned seventeen. I was doing drugs a lot with my friends and staying out late, which was not conducive to being a student. It was the late 60's, and the love generation was completely unruly. Music, love, and drugs seemed to be the important things in life. After I had a couple of bad LSD trips, I made the mistake of telling my mother what was going on with me. She was really scared. Really, I was fine, but my parents got me into psychotherapy by forcing me to go as a volunteer into in-patient treatment. So I went, and I had a wonderful therapist, who realized that I could not go back home. In a short time, I was out of treatment, and I was told I had a choice to either go to a foster family, as my biological family was really not good for me, or I could go to college. The choice was easy. I opted to go to Indiana University.

In the months following leaving home, I had to recover from my general depression borne of being alone and never having been given the extent of love that I felt I deserved. Those depressive feelings are a normal reaction for many young people who are leaving their parents' life. There were also some perks to leaving my parents. Finally, once I had officially left home, I did not have to listen to the negative comments and the shaming that attended most interactions with them.

Only after some time did I realize the real spiritual reasons for my incarnation into this family. Because I knew everything happened for a reason, I knew my stay in this family had to have a reason too. After reviewing all the negative experiences and pain, I realized that I had learned a depth of compassion for people's suffering that could only have come from being harshly treated and denied love. I noticed that my pain had made me look deeper into the reality and meaning of people and events, and it had put a brake on making assessments drawn from surface impressions too quickly.

As I continued to reflect, I uncovered more of the positive lessons I had learned, though these were not easy to recognize at first. One of the qualities that was fostered by our upbringing is that my siblings and I became incredibly independent. I asked myself, "What was I supposed to learn from living in a crowd like this?" The experience of life in my family fostered self-reliance. I did not have to be an island, but I had to concern myself with acquiring whatever I needed on my own. My siblings seemed to be equally challenged to scrape for the things they wanted. Do not get me wrong. We ate well and were adequately clothed. But love was sparse, and attention was measured in crumbs. From age twelve on, I had supported myself through employment. To be able to provide for myself in the area of clothes, food, and entertainment was thrilling to me, actually, and I learned the value of hard work.

Also, under this family regime, I developed a great devotion to the truth and a longing for God. I was not very happy with the way God and truth were represented in the church or in my family. The contrast between the cathedral of nature and my family life was so great, I understood that God's way of doing things had to be different than the hell I experienced being at home. Up until the moment I rebelled at age 12, I was forced to go to church on Sundays and holy days. To me, church lacked joy and was empty of celebration and peace. A wrathful, angry God who dispensed arbitrary judgments on a blemished world seemed much like hell. I rejected this god and this theology.

I yearned to know the truth from experience. Thus, my early life prepared me for and cultivated my desire for the mystical life. The mystical life is the life of real, personal, intense, and powerful experience of the Divine within.

In the following pages, I will explain my own experience of the mystical life, and I will also lay out how you too may experience it.

———————

After leaving home, I worked very hard at many jobs. When I was 18, I married a woman to whom I felt strongly connected and with whom I felt called to a spiritual mission. Then, when I was 19, she and I were at a drive-in movie seeing *Ben Hur*. The scene came where Ben Hur was dying of thirst while being abused and mistreated on a chain gang. A hand appeared almost from nowhere, holding a wooden cup of water for him to drink.

And at once I was that man, dying of thirst and broken by life. I felt that hand of water coming from Jesus was for me, and I fell apart weeping for the pain and losses of my life. I had never before felt as nourished as I did that evening. I was in tears the entire night. This experience of Jesus loving me gave me hope and spiritually brought me to my knees. From that point onward, I knew there was more than what I could see immediately, and I knew I was loved. It was a while before I consciously did anything about that experience.

After working in hospitals for a few years, I then worked in print shops for another few years. Finally, when I was 28 years old, I was meditating and received inner guidance to become a Psychologist. This profession would allow me to really help people one-on-one, guiding them in growing and understanding themselves better. To make it through school while supporting a family, I built and operated a restaurant.

On the courthouse square in Bloomington, Indiana, I leased an old building. It was an old leather shop with barn wood boards floated in concrete on the floor and barn wood nailed to every wall and ceiling surface. Friends helped me with the work. We removed all of the wood and had it placed on a large flat-bed truck to haul it off. We then built the booths, the tables, the kitchen walls, installed the bathrooms, and built a walk-in cooler. After eight weeks, with the help of my wife, I opened the restaurant. I enrolled full-time at Indiana University and ran the business. In 1980, I received my B.S. in Psychology; in 1982, I earned my MA in Educational Psychology; and in May of 1984, I was granted my doctorate in Educational Psychology.

This book will describe the process of developing a real relationship with your inner Divinity. Many people are dissatisfied with present-day "churchianity." Few see God as real or feel that any deep, personal experience of God is possible. Most people feel that God has little to do with their everyday life. In fact, most people, even if they go to church or temple, really do not believe in God. The churches teach that God is something that you can and should be concerned about after you die and are in another place, removed from our three-dimensional life. God is represented as being up in the sky, far away. God is not here and now, permeating our world and our beings.

That idea always seemed wrong and completely absurd to me, even as a child. Only a short, limited view of nature could bring that conclusion. There is a plan and a process of growth for every plant, animal, and human. Careful observation must bring awareness that everything has a purpose. Every human being experiences pain and sadness.

12

Everyone suffers the loss of loved ones and may have been treated badly by those who should have cared about us the most. We have longed to be accepted and known for who we are, but we have been disappointed and abandoned.

This book will give you a way to begin to experience God inside yourself. I will give you some tools to develop your own relationship with the One who created you. What I have discovered is that there is so much more than what we have been taught in our Sunday Schools. There is a fount of wisdom, knowledge, and experience available to all, regardless of education level. All experience is open to anyone, if one receives the proper preparation and training.

Yet, while all experience is open to everyone, not everyone will have identical experiences. We may interpret our experiences differently than others. If several people were asked to get into a swimming pool, each would approach that experience differently. The experience of being in the water would be similar for everyone, but how each person entered the water would be different. Some would get their feet wet inch by inch, some would make a big splash, some would go down the ladder, and some would just fall in with abandon. With spiritual experiences, the same holds true. The approaches may vary, and the interpretations may differ, but the experience would ultimately, essentially be the same. Our interpretation of the experience would be unique primarily because of past experience and training. But what is possible for one is possible for all.

All roads lead to God, however slow and tedious some of them appear to be. My particular path is the way of Christ. "Christ" means anointed. Christ was not Jesus' last name. In early Judean times, his last name was really Jesus ben Joseph. "Ben" means "son of." Jesus was given the name Christ at his baptism in the River Jordan, when he became Christed. In my experience as a disciple on the Christed Path, this path is not the only path to God. There are many.

Applying ourselves consistently and determinately to our efforts in following whatever path we choose decides whether we reach our final destination. Many people feel a resistance to Jesus Christ and his Mother Mary, because the ministers who represent these great Masters on earth have historically been disappointingly troubled and human. Just because a human being fails does not mean that Christ and our spiritual training should be dismissed. We need to separate human frailty from the teachings themselves. Look to the essence of the wisdom of Jesus Christ, and seek to apply your highest understanding to it.

I would invite you to let go of your ideas about the meaning of life and examine the teachings I present to you in these pages. You might be pleasantly surprised. The idea of this book came to me in a meditation, and I was told to write exactly what was given to me. The idea seemed a bit daunting at first, because I have heard the many reactions to religious topics in various circles. However, in comparison to the many mystics of history, my spiritual experiences are not strange or even unique. Many people have had similar experiences. If one person can experience God, then it is possible for all to experience God.

Through these pages, I use words to describe experiences. Sometimes words conceal more than they reveal, leaving room for doubt and speculation about the truth. It is difficult for all of us to describe our experiences, especially if they are fresh and new. You can discover your personal elements of the journey yourself. The map of the territory of our spiritual journey can be fairly accurately drawn and described, but traveling over that path will be very personal. Descriptions are not the actual journey.

This book will show you what needs to be done and how to start on your journey to oneness with your Creator. There is only one Being in whom we live and move and breathe. My prayer for each of you is that you hold your mind open as you read this book and look deep within yourself for verification of what you read. Hold yourself open to see and hear with new eyes and new ears. All the things that the great sages, teachers, and saints experienced, you can experience too. It is up to you. In the process, you will have many trials and difficulties lifted from your life. You will look back, in a short time, and wonder where those troubles went, how it could be that they were lifted from you. People learn in small manageable chunks of information and cannot absorb all the teachings at once. These pages present you with bitesize portions so that you can practice and experience the results in your own life.

The experience of God is not in some distant future in a faraway heaven. The presence of God is right inside you. My purpose in writing this book is to demonstrate this to you. I want you to be able to know the Being who created you and who holds you in everlasting embrace. God's love is so great that when you meet God within yourself, you will be flooded with ecstatic joy and peace. You will know why you are here and what you are supposed to be doing on this planet. Everyone has the same divinity planted within them; it does not get installed when you are "good enough." Your positive or negative actions do not change the way God feels about you. Those negative actions just prevent you from experiencing God and connecting to that presence. God is in you, and God is in everyone else. God is where people are. The old days of isolation in a monastery or hermitage are not useful now. We need to serve God by serving and being with people.

As you read, certain insights will be opened up within you, and you will learn truths that your soul already knows inside. You will remember those things your soul knows and begin to wake up to your spiritual nature. You will begin to understand why you are here on earth and will have many spiritual experiences that will not be speculations or conjecture. You will know. That is very different than belief. I see belief as a grappling hook that people throw into the air, and if it hooks something above them, they stay contented with that awareness. They know something is up there. They have not experienced it yet. They feel it pull when they tug the rope, and so they are contented. That is belief, but it is not the same as an experience. Experience is climbing up there to see that to which the grappling hook is connected. Then you will know something and have true experience of the spiritual life.

CHAPTER ONE
GOD

For, behold, the Kingdom of God is within you.

Luke 17:21

When I was a child, I thought that God was always watching. If I did something wrong, I would be corrected or something bad would happen to me. I did not know any better. I was motivated by fear, so I could not feel God's love, even though I had heard about it.

At nine years old, I had a fully conscious experience of being outside of my body in the middle of the universe, out among the planets and stars, with not another soul around. I was suspended there without needing to use my limbs, and I was aware that I was not inside my body, because I could not directly animate it. I was intensely occupied with the fact that I was all alone inside an eternal universe. Floating there was very exhilarating and exciting, but a feeling came over me that I was doing something too enjoyable to be okay, and I became a little frightened. I remained in this experience for a while and then returned to my body, or, rather, found myself back in my body and joyfully awake.

It was no dream. The next night it happened just as before; I began to feel some anxiety over this phenomenon and decided to check it out with my mother. My mother, a traditional Christian, told me that it sounded evil to her and called it the work of the devil, a pronouncement which caused me great confusion and fear. I wrestled with this dilemma for years. The struggle became an existential one, between my traditional religious upbringing and my direct perception. Only after years of study and training was I able to reclaim this experience and honor it. It was years before

I learned that it was perfectly natural and normal to come and go from my body. This experience, then, was my first direct experience with the living, eternal God.

Because of the struggle surrounding it, the experience fostered an enormous question mark in my mind. Something was happening here, and I did not know what it was. That question alone gave me a burning thirst for the truth which could only be quenched by real experience. I wanted to *know*. I wanted to be sure. I wanted someone to help me learn and discover, and for years, there was no one. My desire to know God grew from that point. As I grew older, I read spiritual texts from many of the world's great religions, and I gradually began to realize that I was not alone in my seeking.

Most philosophers of ancient times began by observing nature and the solar system, looking for interrelationships. Because of their intensity of concentration and desire to know, they became so adept at observation that they began to understand how things worked. They yearned to know the meaning of the phenomena they observed. They trained themselves to be objective, almost standing above or outside of their perceptions. They knew they could influence both perception and matter through their subjective desire, and so they disciplined themselves rigorously to reserve personal bias. This discipline gradually became a pattern of training as it was handed down from teacher to student. Through this method of investigation, the first spiritual schools were created to train students in the same principles of observation. Little by little, they uncovered the answers to some of life's most important questions.

Besides philosophers, there are holy women and men, sages, saints, teachers, and oracles who have led people from the beginning of time. Holy texts are full of accounts of spiritually enlightened people who have a special gift of

18

communion with a being greater than humanity, seers whose job it is to instruct or warn. Every culture has written or oral accounts of spiritual people whose very presence carried instruction and guidance, individuals who were living examples to humanity. These people carried a peace and a presence which seemed to set them apart. Their actions and thoughts revealed a connection with the divine which others lacked. These teachers demonstrated by their presence the reality of something or someone higher and more powerful than we, and they were unanimous on this point: God exists and is aware of everything.

———

There is a story which tells of the time God created humanity. The various aspects of God came together to discuss where to place the divine Self so that it would never be lost. They wanted to make it difficult to find, so that it could not be easily abused. One member of the discussion said, "Place it on the highest mountain." But another said, "No, surely they will discover it." Another aspect of God said, "Place it in the depths of the sea." But it was decided that surely people would explore the oceans and mountains and would discover it. Other suggestions were given which resulted in the same conclusion: someone would certainly find it out.

Then one of them said, "I know where they will never look, where they will not even dream of looking. Let's place Ourselves in the center of the human heart. They will never think to look there." So that is what God did. And to this day, despite the fact that every mystical tradition bears witness to this indwelling presence of God, most of humanity has not looked there.

———

Talking about a God sometimes gets people stuck. Why do we have to call it "God?" Why does It have to be a "somebody?" Cannot It be a "something?" Well, we do not have to call it "God." And perhaps It is a "something." Some people prefer to relate to It as an intelligent, universal energy. Some prefer to personalize It to make It easier to relate to and understand. What one calls It does not change the nature of the being itself. If It exists, then this question is after the fact and will not alter in any way the present reality. He, She, or It probably could not care less what we call It.

Let us suppose there is a God who is powerful and completely aware of creation. Let us also suppose that this God is beyond and above our highest conception, that no matter how we see God, God is always more than that vision, awesome and indescribable. All major world religions and cultures acknowledge the Creator, while they may call It by different names. Some call It Yahweh, some Christ, some God, some Brahma, some Buddha, some Tao, some Mithras, some Ahura-Mazda, etc. A thousand names do not change the Being.

Another question which is often asked is, "Why can't God be a She?" The concept of gender is organic and biological. More importantly, it is archetypal. When it says in the Bible that Man was made in God's image and likeness, the meaning of those words is not that God is a male or female figure physically arranged like us. It does mean that we are made with all of the potential and possibilities of God. We have the same mind, the same love, the same potential consciousness, and the same indwelling priorities in an eternal sense. From God, all human expression becomes possible.

We are spiritual beings with both polarities, masculine and feminine, even if one polarity is a little less expressed than the other. God is both male and female, and at the same time neither. God does care that we acknowledge God, yearning for us to be like God and to be one with God. For purposes of consistency, I will use the words "Father" and "God" to refer to this great being, our Creator, from this point throughout the rest of the book. In reality, God is so pleased to be communicated with at all that God will surely answer no matter how we address God.

Even though all of the serious investigators of God have concluded God's reality, even though God's existence is accepted by millions, even though It is understood as a basic assumption of people's lives, that does not make It a certainty for us personally. What can be said is that we accept this and believe this on faith. This is the purpose of life: to experience God and to allow God to experience through us. God sees with our eyes and hears with our ears. God experiences the trials and tribulations of dense matter through God's specially created vehicle – human beings. All of this created world reflects God and revolves around God and is completely dependent upon God.

This may seem profoundly simple, but there is nothing else. All of our personal plans and schemes are mere compost compared to this grand purpose. So I have to ask you: what does God know through you? What experiences have you allowed God to have through you? Can God see clearly through your eyes, or are your eyes covered with filters and opinions which narrow the view and close the shutters? Can God hear through your ears or is your hearing hardened by wanting to hear things a certain way, rather than the way they are? Can the divine being feel through your heart and really reach out to others who cannot feel God yet? Can God think through your mind and brain? Are God's thoughts going through your mind, or are there myriad confusions passing, ruminating, sloshing about groping for breath?

If God animates and permeates God's own being – the universe – then would not it be reasonable to assume that God already sees all possibilities, knows all inventions, has heard all possible music and seen all art, knowing no limit of time or space? The ambition for originality, that somehow we can create something which even God would envy, is outrageous. It is like trying to outdo the Creator, who is not only the beginning and the end but the process as well. From a human point of view, things can be produced or invented which are new and original. They can be the first of a kind, or the first time anyone has ever seen it.

But from God's point of view, anything "new" to humans existed in God's mind long before we picked it up and reproduced it. The same goes for poetry and music. The best musicians, composers, writers, and poets are the ones who tap into the mind of God and express that through their medium. Then their creations uplift and ennoble us, with the majesty and beauty which alone has God's name on it. What I am saying is not that we will all be the same, that if we get in touch with this creative center within us we will all produce, create, and become exactly alike. That is not how things are set up. The divine being residing within us expresses through us, and this creative force expressing through us produces the genius and beauty of art and science.

In the past few decades, there has been a very energetic push to be different and independent from others. People have gone to great lengths to try to have the newest look, the weirdest approach, the longest or shortest this or that. This tendency to want to be an individual is a great mistake in our culture. Independence encourages people to look to outer appearances, in order to compare how novel or different we are from others, to determine what distinguishes us and ensures our independence. In this way, independence is concerned with only the surface of things. Directing our energies in this way is making us emotionally and physically sick. Very few people have any idea who they are, much less why they are here.

With so much time spent on how we look, how do we have time for asking the more important questions, the kind which I have asked? When all of our material things are put aside, our body is naked, and our hair is shorn off, who are we? What is our purpose on earth? When we are not a conservative, a liberal, an agnostic, a republican, an atheist, a true-believer, a financial genius, a poor person, a this or a that designation, then who are we?

This is the most important search we will ever undertake: to find out who we are and why we are here. Only a relationship with our Creator can supply the missing pieces to that puzzle. Only God has the blueprint and the explanation of who we are and what we are doing here. We have heard so many stories about this great Being that we might be a little confused. Do we really want to focus on this at all? Well, my experience is that God wants us to. God waits patiently for us to pay attention to God. Do not get me wrong. God is fine with us or without us. But both God and we gain from our interaction and the development of a love relationship.

The finite alone has wrought and suffered; the Infinite lies stretched in smiling repose.
- Emerson

A loving father or mother is not diminished by a child's rejection. The child may be completely hostile, and yet the parent still loves the child and desires closeness. The only loser in all of this is the child, who has gone off to be an individual, to be independent. In actuality, we as children of God will never be fully independent. You see, we depend so completely on God that, without God's life moving through our bodies, God's power animating our minds, God's energy causing the blood to move through us, we simply could not sustain life on our own. It is God's ever-present concentration and attention on us that keeps us in God's Being as points of God's consciousness. Without this ongoing connection with God, we would cease to exist.

Many people think that if they can get some kind of unique identity, then they will be recognized as something. They "do not need anybody," but they sure seem to need others to notice them. Let us be honest: we definitely care whether we are wanted, needed, or loved. When it all boils down to what's really important, we want to belong, and we want to love and be loved by someone. Does not this internal longing and desire for union tell us something about how we are built? Does not it tell us something about the One who created us this way?

God created us with all of the longings, sensitivities, and aspirations which are part of God's real nature. God's hand is reflected in our striving to know, to love, to create, to give. These are God's signature and mark upon us. All we have to do is begin to allow these built-in strivings and actions to express, and we will begin to be like our Creator. If we started to be like we suspected God must be, then soon we would have a direct experience of God. In a very real sense, the greatest longing is that of those created for their Father. This longing for God is the original purpose of religion. Each of the religions profess to demonstrate a constructive relationship with God. There are thousands of ways to God – but there is only one God.

Religion is the divinity within us reaching up to the divinity above.
- Ba'Hai Saying

I am in every religion as a thread through a string of beads.
- Krishna, in *The Bhagavad Gita*

24

The word "religion" comes from the Latin words *re*, which means "again," and *ligare*, which means "to tie, unite." So in an essential sense, "religion" means to reunite with God. This is the purpose of all the world's religions, and as such, they are all expressions of our attempt to be "One" with God. It is inherent in everyone to want this. Those who claim no interest have fallen asleep or are bitter about something. Buddhists see the divine in the Buddha; Christians in God or Christ; Hindus in Brahma; the Sufis use Self; Moslems worship Allah; Persians call God Mithras or Ahura Mazda; American Indians call God The Great Spirit. There are a thousand names for the same thing, the same Being.

All revere and worship God with the same degree of longing and awe, with an expansiveness which seems worthy of the One who created us. We need to open our hearts and minds, realizing that each language and culture focuses on and amplifies a different aspect of the One, Eternal Creator. It is also true that if we have a reverence for nature and for people, treating the elements of creation and the people we meet as if they were a part of God, then we have a very spiritual religion.

Ultimately, the issue boils down to one thing: do we have a relationship with this Being, God? Religion is designed to aid us in this regard. But very often, religion focuses on the dissemination of doctrine and disregards the development of a relationship with God. It is sad to see so many people, even those who sincerely seek to serve God, fall short in the area of actual experience of God. They have doctrines, theologies, and words – but little actual communion with God. What is missing in most people's lives is a map of how to become one with God, with this divine center inside them. Your longing for this guidance may have gotten to the point where you read the historical account of some great servant of God and find tears welling up in your eyes, sprung from a well of deep desire in your heart. You look around for someone to guide you in your present era, and you see no one who even holds a candle to someone like Jesus or Buddha. Yet, all of this scrutiny of the spiritual teachings does not bring you any closer to the actual experience of God. Why?

Having gone through the rigors of attaining a doctorate degree, I am considered an educated man. Yet, throughout the educational process, my relationship with God did not develop one iota. Interior work in meditation, prayer, and sacrifice has been the only activity which has prepared and sustained my union with God. God's desire for us to be one with God encourages and fortifies these efforts we make. Academic training is good for intellectual development and for preparing for a career in the world, but the development of the heart and virtuous character demands an entirely different approach.

God cannot be approached through the intellect alone, but instead a deep and abiding longing for God must be present in our hearts. God cannot be figured out intellectually. All of the teachers throughout the ages have taught this. Only through emptying out and giving over ourselves to God can God work us as clay and mold us into what we were originally intended to be. Remember, God has the blueprint, the plan for each of us as a whole being. We can only become whole by being led by God directly and personally. If we try our own method of getting to our destination, we cannot be sure it is God's plan or idea, and we may miss the mark.

When we thoroughly exercise the rational mind, attempting to be a great thinker, there is a good likelihood that we will wake up one day and be proud of our mental output. This pride will grow, until we actually believe we alone created the words that come out of our mouth. We will start to take our ideas very seriously, until soon we have established our god – our mind. This dynamic is true of a lot of things in life.

26

When we take credit for things and begin to possess them, God is left out of the picture. God is not given any credit, and very soon we are alone, holding up the great weight of our conceptions. This temptation plagues each of us, no matter if our chosen area of expression is children, art, music, theology, economics, or whatever else. Either we are doing things for ourselves, or we are doing them for God. Either we are serving ourselves and our own petty little desires, or we are serving God.

A relationship with God is something that grows and develops and requires a commitment. This commitment involves our wanting to know God and be with God. We need to consciously spend time each day with God. It is God's will to be with us, so if our relationship is not growing, it is we who are stopping it. Relationship means regular contact and intimacy and involves the sharing of experiences. This relationship between the Creator and the created is a two-way street: God experiences God's Self through our activities, and we experience God in us. Relationship involves communication. We tell God what we want and how we feel, and God responds with how God sees things and what God wants for us.

This is the point where many people abandon God. They are quite willing to talk to God, but that is where the relationship stops, for they are never quite sure if God is listening. A teacher of mine used to say that God gets a lot of junk mail. I would add that God also gets a lot of requests and questions from people who do not wait around for any answers. Often, God gets the same requests over and over from people who do not have either the patience or faith to listen for a reply. It is *our* responsibility if we do not get answers, because we have not learned to listen.

If we could trust God, then we would know that God would not hurt us or lead us into some abyss. If we could trust God, we would know that God wants the best for us and, like a kind and loving Father, knows us personally and intimately. If this is true, then all we would have to do is to get quiet after we have done some talking, really opening up and listening to the answer God is trying to give us. This listening takes a lot of practice and a lot of mental control, but it can be done. When we truly trust God, we will not have any trouble hearing God's guidance.

We might deceive ourselves if we attempt to answer a particular question with our own ideas. God's direction will make life easier for us in the long run. Pain may be involved in accepting the truth about a situation, but to follow this truth is to save ourselves much more complicated suffering later. The best approach to communicating with God is to be very interested in God's response. Yearn for the truth without holding on to any particular answer, because that is getting you in the way. Leave deciding what is best for you up to God. Demanding that God respond to you in a particular way is going to get you into trouble. We might distort what we hear or see in order to have our own way and miss God's direction in the process.

A relationship with God is very challenging, demanding all that you have and then some. In human relationships, we may be able to convince others that we are right or manipulate them to do as we wish by sheer force of will. Getting in touch with God requires putting aside our own will, thoughts, and desires. There is no way around this. It also requires trusting God, and for most of us, this means overcoming a lifetime of mistrust. Many people have come to believe that they are the only ones who know what is best for them, and they stubbornly cling to this personal myth, living this way all of their lives. Others invest their trust in select people or agencies outside of themselves and deny that God has an interest in them personally. Imagining that God is an amorphous energy outside you that has no personal relationship with you enables you to take little if any responsibility for your part of the relationship with God.

The most difficult obstacle to all spiritual growth is overcoming the programs that parents and caregivers installed in us as children. These tapes may have been placed there with the best of intentions, but often they become the very stumbling blocks which prevent us from trusting God and other people. Even the most well-meaning parent makes a lot of mistakes. Parents are human beings, and so they can be insensitive, mistaking need for love and manipulation for discipline. Human beings are seldom, if ever, consistent. The very nature of being human is to struggle and change, so parents, being human, cannot always be everything they are supposed to be for their children.

Most of us grow up feeling shorted, and perhaps resentful and angry, that mom or dad wasn't loving enough or didn't spend enough time with us. When we get older, we have two choices: we can remain angry and hold on to the past and its deficiencies, or we can resolve to forgive and move on. If we choose to accept our upbringing and understand our parents as imperfect but well-intentioned, we will. How can God become important to us if we are focused on getting our needs fulfilled from an infantile position? How can we trust God, if we feel like our parents still owe us? Why would God even enter the picture, if we are convinced that parents, or people for that matter, are the source of our fulfillment and the satisfaction of our needs? You see, God is not going to be important until we start to grow past these considerations.

God's majesty is present in all things, through God's indwelling, through God's working, and through God's essence. God can therefore be found in all things – in speaking, walking, seeing, tasting, hearing, thinking, and in whatever else we may do. Think of God as the expanse of the universe whose center is everywhere and circumference is nowhere. This entire space is filled with God's mind, God's Consciousness, and it is vitalized with God's energy. Nothing in this entire universe takes place without God's knowledge, and all things transpire in accord with God's plan. I feel some of you thinking that I am getting very close to saying that God's body is the Universe. Well, I am. If we created something out of our own elements and the same substance, mind, and pattern, then that created thing is a part of us.

We are a part of God. Our bodies are part of God, and our divine center is created in God's Image. St. Paul writes, "We live and move and have our being in God." This means that we are a part of God's body and mind. This mind surrounds us and permeates us; we are both in It and of It. This is precisely what philosophers were saying ages ago. They claimed that God and nature were one, and that through nature God reveals God's Self. It is easy to think that God is separate from nature and from our earthly life. We make this separation because we are out of touch with God personally. We do not feel God inside us, we do not feel God's presence overshadow us, we do not feel God's love for us except in some cold, cognitive way.

Part of the responsibility for this confusion must be placed on those who have been the "experts" on God throughout the last few thousand years. They have told us that God is a white-haired, wise gentleman seated on fluffy clouds with radiances emitting in all directions. The wise, white-haired man points his finger and causes the worlds to collide. God is whimsical, irritable, and wrathful. God has our number, and eventually we will get what is coming to us. Another false concept is that accidents and illnesses are caused by virtue of God's random selection. Extending this belief indefinitely forces us to conclude that no matter how we behave, it really does not matter, because there is no order or laws set up to govern our affairs. Another myth created

30

by inexperienced guides is that Heaven is a place which awaits us after we die, that it is unapproachable now, and that, if we please this arbitrary God, we will gain admission.

Every world religion accepts that life is continuous beyond physical death. But the idea of Heaven as blissful happiness and Hell as eternal damnation is something that, years ago, well-meaning spiritual directors found very motivating. Fear is not a healthy motivator, because as soon as we feel better, we slough off until we become frightened enough to get working again. Instead of people being encouraged to be what they truly are, co-creators in the making, they were encouraged to be "good" – which always denotes someone's concept of God. This concept leaves out all spiritual communication with God and makes rules and regulations paramount. Rules and a rigid doctrine have never led anyone to know and experience God. Rules and doctrinal arguments have led to rigid behavior and pride in our own "goodness" – which prevents us from reaching God. Remember, humility is the key to our relationship with God.

Collectively, humanity is beginning to overcome racism, but most people have not gotten over looking at another human being and judging his or her spiritual life or relationship with God. The prejudice that confronts us today is the religious intolerance of what others believe. This is why it is very important not to think more highly of ourselves than we ought. In the New Testament, St. Peter says, "God is no respecter of persons." In other words, God will come close to and be united with whoever allows God to do so. God is not concerned with the boundaries set up between the religions or the other moral criteria manufactured by human beings. It is pompous for us to think that our disapproval of someone influences God's feelings about that person. God speaks to whomever God wants to speak, regardless of affiliation, titles, or function. Thank God that God is not altered by our doctrines and limitations.

Jesus told a story about two people who went into the temple to pray – one a religious man and the other a tax collector. The religious person prayed to God and thanked God that God had made him wealthy, educated, and pious, not like this tax collector. The tax collector prayed to God for mercy for his sins and thanked God for allowing him to talk to him at all. Jesus then asked his disciples which of these two men were righteous before God. They answered correctly that the tax collector was, because he was humble. God does not love us any more if we are good than if we are bad. God's love is perpetual and constant, and we cannot do anything to diminish it. In fact, there is nothing that we can do at all without God.

Which of you by taking thought can add one cubit to his stature?
- Jesus Christ

So what is it that we must do? We must be like God and be one with God. We must think with God's mind, love with God's heart, and create with God's knowing. If we become like God, that will surely suffice to satisfy those who are counting up virtues and adding up qualities, to see if we are good enough.

From a scientific perspective, we are finding out that the universe is so amazingly ordered that we are discovering God on every frontier. The human body, the universe in replica, reflects this divine order. If we were to take our concentration and apply our thinking to reproduce a simple gesture like picking up and taking a drink of water, it would take us much time and effort. If we were to attempt to consciously perform this action, we would have to send signals back and forth each way, from muscles to neuron to brain, hundreds of times in order to accomplish this simplest of tasks. It would be quite exhausting, not to mention time-consuming, to have to do all of this consciously.

The temperature of our planet Earth varies about 150 degrees from season to season, depending on location. Our body temperature can only vary two degrees higher or lower than 98.6 degrees Fahrenheit, or we will die. The ph level of our cells can only fluctuate between 7.0 and 7.8 for us to survive. This is an extremely tenuous and delicate balance. Yet we are surviving within such narrow tolerances. Look at the earth's seasonal rotation. From dawn to dawn each day, the time the earth takes to rotate on its axis varies by only four minutes in 24 hours. This variance requires us to add an extra day onto the year every four years (called a leap year) to account for the difference. Day follows night, night follows day, and seasons succeed one another in stable precession.

Nature has been one of the last bastions of stability for people who have trouble believing in God. At the very least, nature's consistency is remarkable, and few wonder about its permanence. Even scientists tell us the sun will not extinguish for billions of years. I hope you are getting a sense of the magnificence of this divine order. It should be clear from these examples that something much larger and more aware than we has devised and ordered all of this. We are definitely not the Creator. We cannot even explain our own illnesses, let alone why cells divide. We are limited in sight, knowing, and understanding. That is a very humble beginning. From here, we will unlearn many things before we realize who we really are as co-creators with God.

CHAPTER TWO

THE SOUL

And the Lord God formed man of the dust of the ground
and breathed into his nostrils the breath of life;
and man became a living soul.
Genesis 2:7

We are souls clothed with bodies. Our real personality resides in our soul. What we like and dislike, the attitudes and fashions we express, the politics to which we ascribe, all are peripheral to our soul. These attitudes and preferences constitute our individuality and have been developed in this lifetime, through both parental training and interaction with the environment. These influences become habitual behaviors and idiosyncrasies. Our real personality lies deeper than these temporary, superficial considerations. Our real personality, the one based in our soul, contains all our lifetimes of experience, memories, and the associations we gain from them. The soul contains the essence of our experiences recorded permanently, which makes each one of us unique.

When we try to be unique, we are putting on a false self which is not naturally a part of our soul. Our soul does not have to strive to be different any more than the various colors of the light spectrum have to strain to be the color they are. In fact, each soul has a unique hue and intensity reflecting the many experiences it has had from the time all souls were breathed out from the Creator.

The light coming from the soul is not the same as the light which can be seen surrounding a person – that which has been called the aura or atmosphere by some. The aura is a field of electromagnetic energy, mostly colorless, which is made up of the emotional, physical, and mental radiations we are constantly emitting. The aura changes in vitality and color, depending upon our emotional, mental, and physical health. The light from the soul is part of the inheritance given to us by God, and it has traveled with us through our many lifetimes. In contrast, auric emanations are transitory, like moods or mental outlook. The aura is the extension of our spiritual body – which is a mediating energy field between the soul and the physical body.

Mystic philosophers and saints have recorded their experience of seeing the soul over the centuries:
The body is the sepulchre of the soul. All creatures in whom the higher nature is in servitude to the bodily impulses are properly termed dead, inasmuch as truth is dead within them, having no way of manifesting itself....The soul, being immortal, and having been born again many times, and having seen all things that there are, whether in this world or in the other worlds, has knowledge of them all; and it is no wonder that she should be able to call to remembrance all that she ever knew about virtue, and about everything....for all inquiry and all learning is but recollection.
-Plato

Souls never die, but on quitting one abode always pass to another.
- Pythagoras

The Soul is a spark of starry essence. Souls, when they are set free from the body, pass into the Soul of the All, which is akin to them in nature and essence.
- Heraclites

Philosophy is the way to true happiness, the offices whereof are two: to contemplate God, and to abstract the soul from corporeal sense.
- Socrates

Behold, all souls are mine; the soul of the father as well as the soul of the son is mine; the soul that sins shall die.
Ezekial 18:4

From the center of our being outward, we have three distinctly different bodies, each with its own function and purpose. In the innermost center, we have the divine flame, the Word, the Self, the Christ, that part which is God. For the purpose of clarity, I will use the word "Self," although Logos (Word), Divine Fiat, Christ, and Atman are all interchangeable with that term. The Self is a cell in the mind of God, placed within the human soul. This cell connects the soul to the source of all. It is the I Am, that part which was created in the image and likeness of God. This Self is the nucleus of our being, the sun of our microcosm, the power center through which all life emanates into our physical and spiritual bodies.

The Self cannot die and thus is always available, even though it might seem dormant in some people. The soul encompasses the Self, as a shell which protects the Self from interference from the outer world. The soul/Self is you in the deepest and truest sense, the part of you that leaves the body at death and enters the body at birth. This soul/Self will always exist, traveling from life to life and growing evermore able to express God's fullness. This part of you is the Kingdom of God within.

Know you not that you are the temple of God and that the Spirit of God dwells in You?
I Corinthians 3:16

My soul thirsts for God, the living God. When shall I come and behold the face of God?
Psalms 42:2

Before birth into the earth, the soul existed in God's being. The soul cannot remain on the earth without a vehicle, a body in which to manifest. Without a body, it returns to the heaven world to be with God. It is the function of the soul to contain the blueprint for the growth and maintenance of the physical body. The soul holds the archetypal pattern for each organ and cell of the physical body. The soul instructs the developing fetus regarding the attributes which are to be emphasized in the coming child. The genetic components were given at conception through the love of the parents, but the soul orchestrates that development in order to form a body which has the potentials and capabilities needed to carry on its mission and obtain the experiences it requires in its life on earth.

After conception, the soul is responsible for maintaining the autonomic functions of the human body. The heart's diastole and systole, the circulation of blood, the inspiration and expiration of breath, the digestive and eliminative functions, and the hormonal activity are all overseen by the soul. When we sleep, the soul takes over all unconscious bodily processes and regenerates the body, while our brains are quiescent. A number of years ago, a psychology experiment with human subjects was performed in a lab. Volunteers were wired up with electrodes and prevented from falling into REM sleep. REM is the dream state of sleep, which can be seen on EEG (electroencephalogram) monitors (or observed by anyone as rapid eye movements under the eyelids of the sleeper). For seven days, these volunteers were awakened every time they fell into REM sleep. They were being prevented from dreaming, and thus they were prevented from communing with their unconscious.

After seven days, three of the subjects had to be hospitalized in a psychiatric ward, two were in outpatient therapy for months, and one committed suicide. They were experiencing extreme distress because they were not allowed to dream. If we cannot immerse ourselves in the subconscious, we will die. Tapping into the subconscious in dreams is coming into the realm of the soul. The terms "subconscious" and "unconscious" are interchangeable. Yet, unconscious implies a complete lack of awareness of the contents of that part of our psyche. So, since it is possible to be aware of things that are in the unconscious, the term "subconscious" seems more appropriate.

The subconscious mind is the mind of the soul. Our link with the subconscious is that which allows passage of thoughts from our conscious awareness into the soul. Through that same link, messages of the soul pass outward into the conscious mind. The soul guides the development of the brain and body until the individual is prepared to handle direct influence from the soul. In this sense, each soul has its own timing and alarm clock. When the vehicles of body and brain are capable of expressing the pure soul energy, then the person is said to have awakened. There is an old saying, that the angels mourn every soul born on earth and rejoice when a soul dies. This is because, in most cases, birth brings a forgetting of the heaven realm, and death brings an end to the illusion of material separation. In between birth and death, impressions from the soul stream into our subconscious minds in dreams, visions, and intuitions which guide our course and bring us ultimately to the point of realization of the soul/Self.

As we develop, the soul intervenes and steers our course, bringing us into contact with people and experiences in order to bring about spiritual growth. The soul can produce a clear message through a dream, an internal urging, or a vague feeling. The soul is directing and guiding us, whether we acknowledge it or not, and it is responsible for the abrupt changes we experience through the course of our lives. Sadly, most people are unaware of the spiritual nature of life, and so they are out of touch with their souls.

They have forgotten why they are here on earth and what they are to do.

In the process of growing up, our spiritual senses are dulled by parental programming and cultural influences. We are taught that the body is more important than the soul and that all important decisions involve the body. As we mature, our soul becomes covered over more and more by the confusion of a thousand different gods. Our materialistic society reinforces this programming, and it is little wonder that many people no longer concern themselves with whether or not the soul actually exists.

For what is a man profited, if he shall gain the whole world and lose his own soul? Or what shall he give in exchange for his soul?
Matthew 16:26

The soul/Self is the eternal part of us, the only part of us we will take with us when we leave the earth between each life. The Self is a piece of God, placed within each soul when we were created. The soul covers over and surrounds the Self. The Self is the Holy of Holies, the Light within:

The Self is the Rider in the Chariot of the body, of which the senses are the horses, the mind the reins.
- Krishna

The Sun Himself, Who has given it all the splendor and beauty, is still there in the center of the soul.
- St. Theresa of Avila

Behind your thoughts and feelings, my brothers, there is a mighty Lord, an unknown sage. It is called Self; it dwells in your body.
- Zoroaster

At Teigitur I felt and saw, not obscurely, but with very clear perception, the Being Itself, or Divine Essence, under the aspect of a Sun.... After having celebrated Mass, I was praying at the altar, when the same Divine Essence appeared to me anew under a spherical form....
- St. Ignatius of Loyola

Each of these people had the experience of seeing and hearing God within their souls. This experience is referred to as Self-Realization in many schools and religions. Self-Realization is not a cognitive experience, but an actual immersion in the Divine Being. It is not a matter of how perfect we are which determines whether or not we are ready for this experience; it is more a matter of how much we need to know the Self. When the God within us is consciously needed, we will attain Realization, and service to others will be the purpose of our connection with this God within.

You, beloved, also believe that I had every grace with no effort, but this is not so; in fact, I must say that I never received a gift or a favor or virtue without great endeavor and constant prayer, ardent desire, and profound devotion. When we have given God everything we can, although it is very little, God comes to the soul....
- The Blessed Virgin Speaking to St. Elizabeth of Hungary

We are a part of God, of God's encompassing mind, and the Self is God's focal point within us. Around this lighted lamp within, the many layers conceal or reveal the light of the Self to varying degrees, depending on the degree to which we love God and strive to be like God. The Self is our greatest friend; the outer person, as St. Paul called it, is often our greatest enemy.

The realization of the Self is available to all, regardless of religion or cultural background. Some would reject the idea that a person following Mithras or Krishna could be graced with the experience of the realization of God's divine being inside of them. What those people would need to know is that God is no respecter of persons and holds no favoritism with regard to religions. God accepts all people as God's children. Human beings who earnestly seek to find God within themselves will see the Christ residing there and be overwhelmed by the beauty of this experience. It will take much time and effort to bring forth this experience. Do not make the mistake of thinking that your imagination can bring you this experience. Only with the help and guidance of one who has realized God inside can you hope to attain this certainty and peace.

Most people cannot see the soul/Self because negative thinking and acting have caused a film to form on the periphery of the soul. After many years, this negation causes a hardened barrier blocking the light which naturally shines forth from within the soul/Self. This is what the churches call sins, those experiences which separate us from our Creator. Many have allowed their body to be their god, one which rules their lives with despicable tyranny. The Christ light will have difficulty shining through until we voluntarily discipline ourselves and remove the errors in our thinking. In the case of a worldly, hardened individual, it is sometimes necessary for the person to experience a very painful event in order to break the suffocating pattern. When the outer habits become so strong that they choke off the inspiration coming from within the soul, the person is nearing spiritual death. For life to begin anew, something very intense must happen. If the person desires to be one with God, then God will answer this prayer and cause something to occur in his life to wake him up.

When we look at some people's souls, we can see the dark veil of error concealing all but slivers of light. The light is trying to shine forth, but it is prevented from doing so because of encrusted concepts, selfishness, and negation. A person in this state has a soul that looks like an eggshell with cracks all over its surface; only a small amount of light is able to shine through the small cracks in the shell. A soul just beginning on the spiritual path is darkened with a smoky haze. Because of the density of the body and the accumulated error, the soul begins to feel cut off from God and is unable to fulfill its mission on earth. The soul then stirs and begins to wake up the outer person. The spiritual alarm goes off, manifesting as a desire to come home and be one with God. The search begins for like-minded people who are also striving to know God. It is our soul which inspires us spiritually and guides us closer to the Source of our existence.

We must take command of our body and rule it, as a wonderful living machine which will be responsive to our direction. Our love and care will give it the attention it needs in order for it to function properly. The physical body is not evil, but it is like a spoiled child who has been permitted to think that she is the center of everything. The body has been given so much authority over our lives that there will be rebellion when we return control to something higher. The soul/Self is the natural master of our spiritual and physical form; it carries the blueprint of our true nature and function. The physical/animal body knows only appetite and habit, but properly trained, it will be the willing servant of the mind. Whatever the body is trained to do it will do without resistance. It does not have a mind of its own, but it does have a memory. The body is a creature of habit; whatever program we create, it must respond and perform accordingly. Sometimes it takes a concerted effort to change existing patterns, but with time, the body will be happy to oblige. Remember, the real you is the soul/Self. Take charge of your life by turning over the direction of your body and mind to the dictates and guidance of your soul.

Consider the soul/Self as the part of us that is God and the part of God that is us. This is the Master residing within the temple of the human body. What does this Master find when it enters the body at birth? It finds a vehicle which is confining and limited in function, a vehicle which is pure, and clear of any dross, because it has not yet formed any habits which interfere with the Master within. However, as time passes, habits form and fears develop in the child because of its experiences in life. Will the Master within be able to express clearly, as the focus of the new baby moves from God to parents? For years, the Master waits patiently, while only on occasion it is allowed to express through the growing vehicle.

Some human parents are molding the child in their own image and have virtually forgotten about God. Many speak of God or Christ, but they are themselves separated from these divine beings through their own thinking and actions. Parental example often conflicts with the impulses of the Master within. The Master patiently waits for a rebellion by the owner of the vehicle against the thinking of those around him or her, so that the impressions the Master is constantly transmitting can pass into the brain and body. The first experience we have of the transmission of this influence gives us a permanent taste of the Christ mind – and its peace which passes understanding. Once we experience something of the higher reality, we never forget it and long for it continuously. The inner Master supports this longing with subtle inspirations which attract us to people who are also searching and striving.

The interior Master has been imprisoned in a vehicle which does not respond to its love and will not come to it for healing. As long as the temple serves its will to some degree, it will not leave. However, when the lower animal consciousness is allowed to run the show, willfully driving the body and spirit into degeneration, then the Master will vacate the body's walls and cast off the old, imperfect temple. The Master, whose powers are infinite because they are God's, finds itself constricted and confined by the limitations of the vehicle. It is a loving act from the beginning, for this brilliant Master to come into this dense form, a form undeveloped and incomplete. The brain works well, but slowly. The emotions only somewhat resemble the pure feelings the Master feels.

The Master within waits in patience for the hour the mind and heart say to it, "Master, this holy temple is yours. Do with it as you will." This is the point where God begins to inspire us consciously and we do not fight God's direction. Until this time, the Master suffers in its prison, failing to wake up the vehicle's owner to the Divine Source residing within.

Each new experience we have is recorded on our soul. Therefore, the soul grows and changes in relation to the experiences it has. The Self never changes, as it is already complete and perfect. It lacks nothing and has everything. It is part of God. The purpose of our existence is to let God experience the joys and sorrows of dense matter through God's creation – human beings. The more we let go and let God express through us, the more like God we become. God will see through our eyes and hear through our ears and feel with our feelings. God will begin to experience God's creation without interference. As a result, our needs will be taken care of and we will not have disease, confusion, or suffering. All suffering comes from a lack of oneness with God. It is painful being separated from God, and it is painful having to confront our errors and faults on the way back to oneness with God.

A beginning step to finding the soul is to ask God to show us how God sees us. Use the following prayer/meditation to show you what God sees:

"O soul of mine, do reveal me as I am in the eyes of my Creator."

Use this meditation each day, as often as possible, for 15 minutes at a sitting. Do not be afraid if you are shown things that you do not like or do not want to deal with. These are the very things that separate you from God. Only through prayer, meditation, and study of the Bible and other holy books can the soul/Self be found.

I am the way, the truth, and the life; no one comes to the Father but by me.
John 14:6

Jesus Christ was sent by God as the clearest, most perfect Mediator between God and human beings who has ever walked this earth. His job is to draw all souls back to God. God blessed Jesus' mission and expects that we should honor his Son.

All things have been given to me by my Father; and no one knows the Son except the Father, and no one knows the Father except the Son and anyone to whom the Son chooses to reveal God.
Matthew 11:27

By this, we are assured that the Son will reveal God within us when we are properly prepared. The potential of the soul can only be activated by thought, by attention, by longing. Anything we want to know requires us to spend time with it. The laboratory where the soul is discovered is meditation. Meditation brings the outer, animal body into stillness and submission to the higher Self/soul, which allows divine inspiration to pass freely out into waking consciousness.

Meditation is the workbench of all who are serious about their relationship with God. It is the place of greatest communion and the most powerful contact with our Creator. Through meditation, our minds are cleared of debris gathered in the course of our daily activities. Through meditation, we are freed from speculations, opinions, and the impressions of this world. We are open for God to guide and direct us. It allows us to be receptive to God's love and peace.

Meditation is listening to God. We can talk to God, and God will reply in ways that are tangible and real to us. This is not imagination or a pipe dream. We can talk to the Self within, and it will answer. We can see it and hear it, this is a fact. All persons can be trained to do this, if they will let go of themselves sufficiently to allow God to govern their lives, their thinking, and their actions. We do not have to be special, we do not have to be gifted with extra-sensory perception. We just have to be willing. That is simply all there is to it.

The spiritual body is the interim body between the soul and the flesh. It is an electrical matrix of energy which has the same shape and size as the physical body. It is a duplicate of the physical organs and limbs, except its substance is more of light than of dense matter. It is material, but of a much more tenuous substance than flesh and bones. Between the spiritual and the physical bodies are connecting points where spirit and flesh are enmeshed. There are seven of these centers (called chakras in the Eastern religions) which are placed where the sympathetic ganglion connect with major organs or centers in the body. There is one each at the base of the spine, the genitals, the solar plexus, the heart, the thyroid, and near the pineal and pituitary glands. These points are the places where experiences from the body are passed into the soul and where intuitions are passed from the soul to the brain. The spiritual body is responsible for maintaining the health of the physical body, and it actually holds the physical body together.

If there is a physical body, there is also a spiritual body.
I Corinthians 15:44

The spiritual body has the potential to attune itself with other bodies and make itself one with them. In marriage, the spiritual bodies of the two partners become united as their love deepens and grows. The spiritual bodies can be tied directly to each other during a marriage ceremony, through the words of the sacrament, or this unification can happen over time. It is the spiritual body which enables us to feel what others are going through and empathize with them.

The soul is placed within the spiritual body, in the vicinity of the heart. From this center within the body, emanations of God's energy and light flow out through the spiritual body into the flesh. When there is no resistance to God's energy, the body is filled with vitality and life; when the thinking of the brain and the bodily desires cloud over the pure influences of the soul, then the spiritual body is prevented from transmitting these energies from the God within and thus vitalizing the flesh. Our waking decision means life or death for us, spiritually speaking. God cannot force God's way through and burn out the dross of our life of habits, unless we invite God. We are free to make choices. And of course the consequences of those choices are definite and precise. In very severe cases, when we choose to cut off the spiritual energies coming from within, we will die a spiritual death, which has the potential to gradually progress to the death of the body.

The soul/Self is continuously sending out waves of light and life from the center of our being. If we would think less and let go more, we would experience this fully. Since we are generally our own worst enemies, we tend to block this light and love from God and cut ourselves off from the Source. The spiritual body is left to try and repair the damage to the physical body, which is caused by this cutting off of energy. Most disease and sickness is caused by the shutting out of God's healing energy through our limited thinking and selfishness. The spiritual body is never affected by disease – it is always in perfect form. Yet, to ask it to maintain the health of the physical against the odds of continuous negative thinking is more than it can do. In this case, we have made a decision (conscious or unconscious) to cut ourselves off from God, and nothing can be done until that decision has been changed.

There are people who have had a limb removed who report sensation in the extremities for months or years following the procedure. Physicians say this phenomenon is because of the nerve endings being accustomed to firing all the way to the end of the limbs. But in actuality, the sensations are caused by the spiritual body, which is still intact and being sensed by the individual. The spiritual body is electrical, much like our nerve energy, and it is keenly sensitive throughout the body. The spiritual body atrophies much more slowly than does the physical, which is why the sensitivity exists in parts that are not physically there.

A number of times, I had an experience of the spiritual body on waking from sleep and finding that I had slept on my arm in some restricting way. I would experience a feeling of numbness and not being able to move my arm. Then, I would find my spiritual arm floating straight down through the mattresses into the floor at an angle which would have been physically comfortable. I could see and feel the light in my spiritual arm, as it floated there. I would invariably become concerned that my physical arm was dying without blood flowing into it, so I would gradually move my spiritual arm back to mesh into the physical. At this point, I could again feel tingling and blood moving. It is much the same with moving in and out of the physical body in dreams or in meditative states. We carry the spiritual body and soul with us as we move in and out. The physical remains still and relatively inactive, except for the functioning of the autonomic system.

There are as many names for the spiritual body as there are for the soul. Here are some of the most commonly use names: vital body, causal body, astral body, etheric body (although this is a little more like an emanation from the physical), and prime body. These all are interchangeable terms. Some teachers have even described the spiritual body in terms of many different levels or degrees. This complexity is unnecessary and only confuses people. We can observe different levels of intensity of the light in the spiritual body, when looking at different people. How much we can see is dependent on their spiritual development and how much of God they let move into their waking consciousness; the more developed the soul, the more observable the levels.

Russian researchers have been studying the electrical emanations given off by plant and animal life for years. Actual photographs have been taken of the various radiations of light which surround parts of people and plants. The fact is scientifically proven that light is being radiated out from all animate and inanimate objects. The greatest portion of light energy is radiated from human beings, as judged from their photographs. This should not surprise us. If the Dominion of God is within, then there is a source of power, force, and life radiating inside of us. All we have to do is tap into it and permit it to shine forth into our world.

At the physical death of a human being, the spiritual body gradually atrophies and dissolves, but after a much longer time period than the decomposition of the physical body. The spiritual body is only required for manifestation in a material, earthly body. Otherwise, the soul/Self is all that we need to be with God. The spiritual body is the opposite polarity of the physical. If you are male, then your spiritual body is female in polarity; if you are female, then your spiritual body is male in polarity. In a sense, then, spiritual marriage takes place on two levels – both physical and spiritual.

I bring this element of the polarity of the spiritual body up for discussion because men and women approach God differently. A man cannot reach God unless he gives over, lets go, and submits to being guided and directed by something higher than himself. He needs to approach God by being receptive and passive. He has to become nothing in order to reach his own soul/Self. A woman cannot be passive and ever hope to reach God. She is naturally receptive, and thus she must create a connection with God which is decisive and dynamic. She must seize her contact with God in an active way. For a man, the greatest stumbling block in his pursuit of God is his ego and overcoming a false sense of self-sufficiency; for a woman, the greatest stumbling block is her tie to the earth and overcoming complacency. I am speaking generally here and am aware that exceptions can be found to these basic guidelines.

Once we have approached the Self, through our soul and spiritual bodies, the concept of male or female becomes irrelevant and meaningless. Being one with God requires our becoming points of light and life which are neither male nor female, but both. God is neither and both at the same time, because within God are all vibrations of the spectrum. In the material world, we have determined that spiritual things are of God and material things are evil. But this is not the case. Matter is merely the part of the Spirit of God which manifests to our senses and is perceivable to us. Matter is not evil or bad, nor is it separate from God. God animates all space, time, and matter. God's signature is everywhere, and God's presence fills the entire universe. When God created all of this, God said it was good. Our task here is to manifest God through our soul, and our spiritual and physical bodies, so fully that there is no separation in mind or action between God and us. The spiritual and physical bodies are our energetically stepped-down vehicles to enable us to manifest as souls here in this material plane of vibration.

If finding the Self and becoming the soul is what we desire above all else, then we must put all material considerations to one side. Leave all religious, philosophical, and mental speculations on the shelf while you devote your entire attention to your direct contact with God. Spend time with prayer and meditation every day. Do not spend hours and hours – just twenty minutes or so in the morning and evening. That amount of time in prayer and meditation is sufficient to change your entire life. Read inspirational books, the Bible, and other sacred works. Keep your thinking clear of anger, resentments, selfishness, and negative attitudes. A remarkable transformation occurs in people who simply clean up their thinking, replacing their negative thoughts with positive, joyful ones.

If you want peace, pray for it to enter your body and mind. Then act peacefully. Continue to monitor whether you are being peaceful or not. If agitated, make contact with God so peace will be yours again.

ξ

CHAPTER THREE

PRAYER

Ask, and it will be given to you; seek, and you will find; knock, and the door will be opened to you. For the one who asks always receives; the one who seeks always finds; the one who knocks will always have the door opened to him.

Matthew 7: 7-8

A number of years ago, I found myself out of work, and the experience provided me with a lesson which I will never forget. Prior to that period, I had never had trouble finding employment; in fact, it usually took only two or three days to line up some work. This time, I found that two weeks had passed since I had worked, and I was beginning to be distressed. I had followed my usual procedures of making a prayer and scouring the classifieds, but otherwise, I stayed at home waiting for the phone to ring. I discussed this with my spiritual director, and he gave me these instructions: "Tomorrow morning, wake up at 7:00 a.m., have breakfast, pack your lunch, and hit the streets, putting in an application at every business until you find a job."

The next morning I made my prayer, asking for God's help in finding a job, packed my lunch, and went out as instructed. By lunch time, I had knocked on countless doors, filled out innumerable applications, and had found nothing. So I sat down by a canal in the center of that southern California town, to renew my strength. I felt like I had already worked half a day, and, as my faith was becoming a little wobbly, I reaffirmed my prayer of the morning. I recalled that my adviser had told me that "my job was to get a job," and that I was to continue looking from 8 a.m. - 4:30 p.m. each day until I acquired one. After lunch, I forged ahead in my resolve and walked into a natural foods store. Not only was I hired on the spot, but I was given work which I enjoyed and at a higher rate of pay than I had expected. This lesson was expressly clear to me – if you want something, step out on your prayer in faith as if it is being handed to you. Prayer is a matter of asking God for what you want and then putting yourself on the line to receive what you have asked for.

For most people, a prayer is a series of words or phrases which communicate beautiful ideas to God. Prayers are perhaps the simplest things to compose, yet many people seem to have a block about how to do so. There are numerous books which list prayers by category, for people to repeat if they have trouble creating their own. Some of these prayers are sculpted with artistic attention, so that we can give something beautiful to God. Unfortunately, very few people can speak frankly to God, as they would a friend. Many lack the courage to have a heartfelt, concentrated conversation with God.

Many people are afraid to talk directly to God. They fear that God might become angry if we are not respectful enough, and so they are concerned about drawing God's attention in their direction. If we have offended God, then surely God will remember to give us some series of calamities when it crosses God's mind. Others worry about interrupting God's busy schedule, feeling the relative insignificance of their needs in relation to the rest of creation. Often, we fear that if we actually experience a contact with God in prayer, God will want us to become religious, holy and pious, giving up all of our worldly enjoyments. Perhaps God will want more from us than we are willing to give.

Prayer involves a relationship between ourself and our Creator. For the most part, this relationship has not been developed in the past, because prayer has been a laborious practice done out of sheer desperation or absent-hearted

54

obligation. Often, we pray and we do not feel that we get a response from God that we consider definitive or real. Even when a prayer is answered, we often do not acknowledge God's hand in it and choose to explain it away as coincidence.

The tragedy is that many of us were taught as children to thank God for what we have and to ask God to fill our needs – but then we left those practices in our childhood. Our relationship with God has not grown and matured, because few people know how to teach us how to grow and mature in our faith. Unfortunately, priests and other religious leaders have not been able to teach us, either. They may speak eloquently of God, they may have great faith and a deep understanding of the scriptures, but do they know God? Have they felt God's presence and heard God's voice? Can they teach anyone else how to come to know God? We want to *think* more than we want to truly *know*, and so, through lack of persistence, patience, and working with God's Laws, we have settled for intellectual comprehension, instead of a dynamic relationship with the living God.

Why would God set up a creation where God could not communicate with or inspire God's creation? Would God want to make it one-sided, with people able to talk to God but not hear God's response? Or, the other alternative, where God only spoke and was not interested in hearing us speak to God in return? The reality is that God communicates to whoever is open to God. Thousands have heard God's voice, distinct from their own mind or voice. Thousands have spoken to God and have been certain of God's response. When an individual has this experience, it is no longer merely a matter of belief that God answers prayers; instead, God's answers are a reality that is known in the deepest and truest part of one's being.

Often people feel that this business of prayer has strings attached to it. Please reread the quotation at the beginning of this chapter, and reflect on what it says. This scripture makes no mention of whether God approves of what we are asking for, nor is there mention that God will answer our prayer only if we ask for things which are of a virtuous or spiritual nature. The passage simply says that what we ask for will be given to us. This is a concept which may be difficult to understand and which may run counter to instruction we have been given. We may have been taught that God weighs our requests before deciding to answer them. In other words, we might have been taught that God takes responsibility for the things we ask for and protects us from ourselves and our limited thinking.

This belief deserves careful consideration. Most likely, we have wanted things in our life that have proved to be unhealthy, or perhaps even damaging to ourselves or others. We may have wanted material things that we did not need, but we were able to obtain them through our own efforts and persistence, and God did not keep us from them. We may have wanted things which were not appropriate, reacting in the heat of anger, and yet God did not intervene. God does not exist to stop us from doing what we want. God wants us to make our own decisions and take responsibility for their natural consequences. How can we grow, if we do not make mistakes and learn to discern what is or is not good for us?

God is very much a wise and loving Father. The consummate considerate One, God will never force God-Self on us, nor intervene unless invited to do so. Although God has instilled in each person the freedom to make choices, inevitably, time will prove God's absolute dominion over our affairs. God does have an overall plan, but God leaves the day-to-day living to us. This is the way we learn and the way we grow. We are free in our choices; we are also free to experience the results of our decisions. God will not make us love God; God will not force us to seek contact with God.

God waits for us to volunteer. Our love for God has to come from within our own heart.

Do we think that what we do does not have an effect? Why does God give us a choice and let us pay the consequences? When we want something, that desire makes an impression on the mind of God and is automatically returned to us in a more developed form. Our every thought has the power to invoke this Law which is inherent in God's being. Even the laws of matter state that for every action there is an equal and opposite reaction. In other words, everything we think, say, or do sends energy out in a particular direction, and that energy is destined to come back to us over time. This teaching has been an important part of many religious systems down through the ages. Jesus illustrated this Law when he declared that our word would not return to us void. The Old Testament teaches that as we sow, so shall we reap. The Hindu doctrine of karma teaches that we get back what we put out into the universe. The reaction might be quick or slow, but this is the way the universe is designed, and there is no escaping it.

God set up the plan as the great Architect of this system we live in, and God created human beings in God's image. God's design includes some basic patterns or laws. We are free to have whatever we desire, but we must live with those choices. We end up paying for wanting things that are harmful to ourselves or others, and even so for those things that are not essential. Energy is infinitely available to all of us – energy which we can use constructively or destructively. God leaves the decision up to us. When Shakespeare wrote, "There is nothing good or bad, but thinking makes it so," he was implying that it is people who declare a thought or action good or bad, depending on how it is subjectively viewed. What appears to be good may not be so in reality. What appears as evil is very often a blessing in disguise.

Take lightning for example. It can kill us, or destroy trees and buildings – or it can hit a lightning rod and purify our water supply. If it kills or destroys, we declare it to be bad. If it clarifies the water supply, then we say that it is good. The energy and essence of the lightning is the same. But it is how that energy is used that determines whether we see it as good or bad. We are used to looking at things shortsightedly. We hear of hurricanes and earthquakes, and we say that they are horrible. Ultimately, these natural disasters often serve to bring nations together in working to help one another. Then we can decide that they are good. We need to examine this good and bad idea and attempt to see how God sees. God is a good Father who knows that through trial and error, we will come to learn. We will begin to see that pain and suffering are caused by desiring what is not necessary, as Buddha taught.

Our problems come from not knowing who we are, from wanting what is not compatible with our real nature. Our true nature is God's nature – God's Image and Being within us. We were created by God, and we reflect God through our creativity and feelings. When we strive to know God, and we make the effort to be with God, we begin to know ourselves in the most profound sense. We are all responsible for our actions, whether we choose to be conscious of God's Law or not. We inevitably will reap what we sow. It is just a matter of time before we come face to face with the consequences of our actions and choices. If we deny our responsibility for the things in our life, the lessons will need to be much harder, and they will be repeated over and over until we learn them. You see, God wants us to be like God. If God handicapped us by taking freedom of choice away, we would never be able to know what it is like to become one with God.

Prayers that are not clearly formulated and directed to God take longer to be answered, because they are not focused or developed. If we are not clear that we want something, or have conflicting desires, then our prayer is confusing and will take longer to resolve in our mind. It is as simple as this: when we decide, then it gets done. If we are not sure if what we want is good for us, or if we know it is not good for us, we will not put the full conviction of our desire before God. We may feel hesitant or ambiguous about wanting something, especially if we want something for someone which may violate that individual's freedom. If our doubt is strong enough, it becomes a prayer. An unclear prayer will reap an unclear response.

There are spoken prayers, and there are silent prayers. The unspoken prayers of the heart are often the most powerful, because often, the desire behind them is more intense and clear. God is especially responsive to these innermost prayers. We need to realize that we are transmitting messages into the mind of God all the time, and these messages are picked up and acted upon by the universal energy of God. The simplest definition for prayer is talking to God. You communicate with God just like you are talking to a person next to you. It is much like picking up the telephone and dialing the number of your friend. The friend picks up the receiver, and you can feel and hear that someone is on the other end of the line before the friend says anything. You will feel you have made contact with God in the same way. You will know that somebody is present and listening to you. Then, start to speak what you want to say to God.

The conscious use of God's Law through prayer is a skill, and, like any other skill, it develops with practice. There is a basic procedure to follow in prayer, one that can be thought of as a scientific method. If something is scientific, you can follow the given procedure and get similar results each and every time. Here are the steps to scientific prayer:

Step 1

Decide what you want to create. Get a clear picture in your mind of what you want, and make sure you really want it. The clearer you are about what you are praying for, the clearer will be your response. Your image must be free of all ambiguity and beyond the shadow of any doubt.

Step 2

Make contact with God. Get quiet and ready to talk with God, and then hold a space open inside yourself until you perceive that contact has been made. To do this, you must be free of all unrelated thoughts and desires. Often, there is an instantaneous response. You may feel that God is there with you as a presence, as a sense of peace, or openness to a higher reality. Or you may perceive an increase in the light on your inner visual screen as you look within.

Step 3

Ask for what you want. Tell God what you are thankful for, and share with God how you feel. State what you need, either inwardly or verbally. See the fulfillment of your prayer as a clear mental image, with all of the movement, color, and texture of which it is composed.

Step 4

Accept what you have asked for. Let go of your prayer, releasing it into the Mind of God. Thank the Creator for listening, and turn the prayer over to God. Allow the creative intelligence of God to handle the timing and means of your prayer's fulfillment. Do not think about it or wonder when it will happen – just know that it will be taken care of and that it exists as a creation in the mind of the Creator. To help you visualize the process, imagine that the prayer was a package of light which was placed before God. Visualize an angel coming to pick up the package and deliver it to God to be answered. As the angel carries off your light creation, let go of it, knowing that you must release it before it can return to you in its manifest form.

If you follow these steps faithfully, your prayers will be answered. This method of prayer implies that we can do nothing by our own limited abilities and understanding. Everything that we do takes energy, and that energy is God's. God animates our thoughts and actions by God's power. Without God making that possible, we would not exist. God wants us to have this infinite Source of power and energy at our disposal, so that we can experience God. It is God's will that we become co-creators with God. As we gain experience with prayer, we learn to be familiar with the way God creates and to take responsibility for our creations.

Prayer makes you the navigator of your own destiny, giving you back control over the affairs of your life. Prayer puts you back at the helm, awake and able to steer the ship to its destination. So many people feel that they are like corks bobbing around in a vast sea of confusion – they do not know where they are going and are not sure if they can keep afloat. As they bob around on the whimsy of the waves of the world, there seems to be no relation between causes and effects in their lives. Consequences remain unrelated to choices they have made, and thus life appears to be volatile and reactive.

Life does not have to be like that. Through the conscientious use of prayer, you can reclaim your rightful relationship with God, stripping away unconscious concepts which bring the feeling of being at the mercy of the world and its whims. God is not arbitrary or irritable, nor does God govern creation by emotional whimsy, doling out punishment and reward at random. God has set up this universe with immutable, scientific laws which we can rely upon. Prayer is just one of these laws. According to these laws, if you want something enough and release it to the Creator, it will be done. Our thought and desire creates a vacuum, a space for God to fill. We have the right to choose what we will. It is up to us what we want to create and accept into our life. But it is the power of God that manifests it there.

You opened your hand and satisfied the desire of every living thing.
Psalms 145:16

Is there a man among you who would hand his son a stone when he asked for bread? Or would hand him a snake when he asked for a fish? If you then, being evil, know how to give your children what is good, how much more will your Father in heaven give good things to those what ask God!
Matthew 7:9-11

God's energy will work on any prayer and answer it for you. It does not matter if the prayer is positive or negative; it will be answered. The Law is activated both by conscious thought and by subconscious thought. The individual who habitually talks about calamity coming into his life and who fears impending disaster and illness is creating an unconscious prayer for the very things he fears. Our doubts and fears are prayers, too. Doubts are simply faith placed in the wrong things. In truth, every thought we have and every desire in which we clothe our thought becomes a living prayer and has the power to activate God's Law. The truth of this Law is why Jesus taught that an individual who thinks about committing adultery is actually committing adultery in his heart.

The Law of God is in operation all the time; we are always receiving answers to our prayers, even though we may not

62

be following the formal steps outlined earlier. We might be angry at someone and want things changed in a relationship; we might want to get back at someone; we might need to feel like we belong; we might long for someone to talk to; we might need help with the mortgage payment. These are prayers spoken in the confines of our own heart and mind. These unspoken prayers of the heart and mind are answered by God just as precisely as the formal ones. The only difference between the two forms of prayer is that the formal, scientific prayers clearly acknowledge God and God's awesome authority over our lives. With practice and experience, our use of this creative Law will grow to be much more conscious and reliable.

Most people fill their minds with thoughts which debilitate and tear down people and life. One of the most painful gifts to have is the ability to read minds and pick up other peoples' thoughts. Often, I have been given to know what someone is thinking without attempting to read his or her thoughts. The impression usually comes out of the blue. First, I am startled by a thought which has entered my mind, and then I realize it is coming from another. The way I can tell this is so is that the thoughts are usually not something I think about, and they have a quality that is unfamiliar to me. These thoughts represent unfulfilled desires and needs which are actually prayers. Sometimes we are not even sure what these unfulfilled desires and needs might be. When we are not sure what we want, we live our lives on hold waiting for something to happen. This style of life is not creative and does not take responsibility for our experience.

If we make a prayer for something, faithfully following each step, and the prayer does not manifest as we expected and hoped, what went wrong? Well, part of us might have wanted the prayer to be fulfilled . . . but another, stronger part may have been resisting it. This is why it is important that we be free from ambiguity and know what we want beyond the shadow of a doubt. The realm of the shadow is the subconscious; often we have desires and thoughts out of conscious range which are more powerful than our consciously held beliefs.

When our prayer was not answered, perhaps part of us might have believed that we were not worthy of having our prayers answered. The interference to the prayer's fulfillment might have been as simple as doubting ourselves or our ability to pray or contact God. This doubt, if strong enough, becomes the overriding prayer, and it is answered like all other things in which we have faith. Most people have more faith in their doubts than in their ability to hope and see those hopes realized. If you want two things at once, the stronger conviction or prayer will be answered. Thus, if you have greater doubt that hope and faith, the prayer of that doubt will be realized. It is that simple.

A house divided against itself cannot stand.
Mark 3:24

This is why it is important to get a clear mental picture of what you want before you pray, so that nothing will be in the way of your prayer being answered and manifesting in your life. Sometimes these doubts are very subtle, and it is hard to determine what is causing the alteration in your prayer. Years ago, one of my brothers had been taught this scientific step-by-step approach to prayer, and he decided to try it out. He prayed for a Porsche, visualizing all of the details of model and color, asking for what he wanted, and then he thanked God for having heard him. Within three days, he had the fulfillment of his prayer. His girlfriend brought him a Porsche which exactly matched all of his visualized specifications – with one exception: the Porsche was only three inches long. He had neglected to visualize the car's size. This is a humorous example, but it emphasizes an important point. What you have in mind when you pray is critically important in determining what exactly you are going to receive.

Also, if you have stronger, over-riding prayers for yourself or for your life, God may answer these before individual prayers that would conflict with your overriding prayer. I know a man who spent a whole year wondering why he could not find employment. He prayed for a job with specific pay, good benefits, and prestige, one which would challenge him and would make use of his skills. He went to many interviews for jobs that seemed promising – but each time, he was turned away. He came to me one day in frustration, and, as we talked, he shared with me that he did not want a job which would so occupy his ego that he would forget his spiritual striving. His faith was very strong, I discovered, that God would steer him away from a job which might interfere with his spiritual growth.

It was clear to me that this prayer, his real, strong prayer, was being answered. He had forgotten the important condition which he himself had set up in his prayer. The jobs for which he had been interviewing would have been so distracting and demanding that he could have felt lost within the year. The real prayer, his underlying intention to remain dedicated to his spiritual growth, was the most powerful prayer, and it had been answered. All prayers are answered. We simply are not always aware of the most important prayers our hearts are broadcasting into the Being of God. God satisfies his creation continuously and without fail.

In everything, by prayer and supplication with thanksgiving, let your requests be made known to God.
Philippians 4:6

The surest way to get to know God and yourself is to pray. Pray for things that you want, simple material things at first. This may sound a little foreign to your thinking, if you think God would not deign to supply our simple material wants and needs – but remember, God animates this world with God's Intelligence. God is not separate from our material existence, or God would not be able to fulfill our material needs.

A number of years back, our family was in need of money to pay our rent. I had been temporarily out of work, and my wife was not making enough to support us. In desperation, I prayed for $300, so we could pay the rent. I did not tell anyone else about this prayer, because I was ashamed of not being able to provide for my family. One day before the rent was due, I came downstairs and found an unmarked envelope under our front door. In it was $300. Within that experience, I was overwhelmed by the power of prayer, and I have never forgotten that lesson. God has absolute power over the material Universe and will get us what we really want, if we will only ask God for what we want.

I want to establish clearly that I am not promoting using the Law of Prayer as a way to get rich. The Law can do that for you – but being wealthy carries a responsibility which you may not want, or which you may not be strong enough to handle. When I was a teenager in the 60's, I looked around and concluded that power and money seemed to be at the root of all of the corruption in society, and I made a decision, a prayer, that I would have no part of either. For the next nine years we were poor. We always had what was absolutely necessary, but not much more. We lived out of orange crates and trunks, with furniture we bought at Goodwill stores and rummage sales. This lifestyle was sufficient for us for many years.

When later I learned to pray effectively, this fear of what money could do crept in again. I spent a whole month wrestling with this fear. Through that struggle, I realized that, for me, not having money was safe – that as long as I did not have any, I did not have to be responsible for using it wisely. Also, I concluded that money itself does not make people corrupt, but instead it is our undeveloped character which makes us use money irresponsibly. Money is a medium for getting a lot of things accomplished, and it is a means of exchange between people on earth. Once I became clear about this issue, our income increased three-fold in less than two months. My underlying prayer of restriction became a prayer of acceptance, and my income reflected my change in attitude.

A word of caution. The Law of Prayer is activated by our thoughts and desires, but it is also necessary to demonstrate our acceptance of it through action. We must be willing to be the avenue through which the prayer works. For example, if you need a job, and you wait by the phone or for an invitation by mail, you may be waiting a long time. You have to go out and make yourself available by putting in applications, making phone calls, and calling on businesses. This gives God something to work with, and it demonstrates your commitment to have what it is you asked for. In both your thoughts and actions, you need to demonstrate your willingness to accept the fulfillment of your prayer.

The heartfelt prayer of a good man works very powerfully.
James 5:16

The use of prayer is a school for learning about the world and ourselves. When we obtain things that put us out of touch with ourselves and our Creator, life becomes miserable. But the resultant pain brings the wisdom necessary to remove these conditions from our lives. Often, the intensity of the pain will goad us to take the necessary steps to change the situation. Ask yourself – is it more painful to keep a problem or to relinquish it?

How you answer this question determines your readiness to change. So often I see people so weighted down with troubles and sorrows that they appear physically stooped over. What is amazing is that, when offered help and the possibility of removing those burdens, they often refuse to have them lifted. Many people cling to their tribulations and difficulties, because they are familiar. Without these problems, they would no longer know themselves, and they would feel purposeless and naked if stripped of them. Afraid of what life would be like if they changed something, they hold on to their pain like it is their livelihood.

Prayer can make possible what we think is impossible, because it puts us at the point of cause. If we believe that the events and situations of our life occur randomly, then we will not be able to take responsibility for what we have created. People blame God for things that happen because they forget that they themselves set in motion what they are experiencing. Prayer gives you the ability to mold your world and your life in accordance with God. Pray for little things at first, things which can be materially manifested to you. Let God take care of the results. In this way, you can gain trust in God, and you will grow stronger in knowing and faith. Then, pray for the big things in your life, as your faith deepens and you become more familiar with how prayer works.

The principle of prayer from a scientific point of view is simply this: NATURE ABHORS A VACUUM. Scientifically, every vacuum is filled. Your prayer creates a vacuum, which God's Law always fulfills. If you ask for someone to receive a blessing, you are creating a vacuum for that person which God will fill. The blessing could consist of seeing the person whole, happy, or healthy. You could see a person healed of a disease and ask for this to be done for them. You need only have faith that what you ask for will be done, and it will be.

Whatever we make a space for, through our need and our wanting, God will fill that space. If you want problems, hold them before God, and God will make the ones you have larger and more pervading for you. If you want to be whole, lay that desire of your heart before God, and God will fulfill your wanting. God's Law is impersonal and will always fulfill your prayers – whatever they are. In the words of St. Paul, "Pray without ceasing." Know that your every thought, desire, and action is a prayer.

ॐ

CHAPTER FOUR
MIND OF CHRIST

*Let this Mind be in you which was also in Christ Jesus, who,
being in the form of God, thought it not robbery to be equal
with God.*

Philippians 2:5

In Zen monasteries, a student is often given a riddle called a koan to solve. The word "koan" means, literally, "a precedent-establishing formulation." A koan provides a point of focus for the mind while at the same time posing an impossible paradox. The student is instructed to concentrate on the riddle, to keep all thoughts still and the mind free from distractions. In order to solve the koan, the mind must transcend its own thinking, making a jump across the synapse which separates the intellect and direct perception. In this way, the deeper meaning is discovered in the present moment.

This exercise is designed to frustrate the conscious mind to the point of surrender, bringing enlightenment through direct perception. When we hold the mind still, we allow inspiration and revelation to arise from within our divine center. Accomplishing this is the purpose of meditation, and it is essential to all spiritual development. Gaining control over the mind is the first essential step of spiritual unfoldment.

The first consideration in developing some control over your thinking is to learn the art of concentration. Concentration means thinking about one thing and that one thing only. It means the ability to focus one-pointed attention without the interference of distracting thoughts. It is vitally important to develop concentration if you ever want to hold your mind quiet enough to allow God to speak to you and guide you. This silent mind can be likened to a body of water completely still and transparent – no quivering, no anxiety, no restlessness. In this stillness, we watch and wait, having placed our cares and worries aside. This is a receptive state, arrived at after all concepts and opinions are dropped and the mind is open and clear.

Without concentration, there is no prayer, no meditation. In our present world, television is training us to be attentive for shorter and shorter periods of time. Media experts know what sells and how long people can remain interested. Very few people can concentrate on a single thought for more than a few seconds at a time. So commercials get shorter and shorter, as people's attention spans decrease.

You can assess your ability to concentrate by trying this simple exercise. Place a regular orange in front of you on a table, about 1 ½ feet away. Examine it slowly, studying its surface, keeping your mind on it, and do not let any thoughts or fantasies distract you for three minutes. Set a timer, so you will not wonder what time it is or how long you have been concentrating. Be very demanding on yourself! Did any thought come in which was not directly related to the orange? Did you find your mind wandering to other things? Did you see yourself looking at the orange and feeling a bit foolish? If so, then you were letting yourself be distracted, and during those moments you were not concentrating. If you feel the need to train your mind further, you can try the following exercise.

Again, place an orange on a table in front of you. This time you can set a timer for 15 minutes. Examine the skin of the orange, the color, the smell, the shadows, the texture, and the shape. Do not touch the orange and do not ponder the philosophical meanings of this exercise. Simply look at the orange, focusing on its surface and keeping all other thoughts out. Then, allow your eyes to look into the orange, penetrating the skin; see the pulp and the membranes of each section. See the little sacks of juice, the strands which tie these little nodules to the middle spine of the orange. Then look at the central spine of the orange, noting its color and texture. Look closely at every part. The more you are able to focus your mind, the more you will actually be present inside that orange in your mind's eye.

Now, take a seed which you find in one of the sections and examine its many layers. Explore its rough outer skin and the finer, softer skin on the inside. Find the white body of the seed. Inside of this seed is the germ of potential life. Take the seed and see it planted in the fertile earth, warmed by the sun and moistened by the rain. See it growing up, sprouting out of the earth, reaching up to the sun. See the sprout develop leaves and become a seedling, the seedling growing more full and bearing branches and leaves. See the trunk growing steadily and the tree maturing, eventually producing fruit. Pick an orange from the tree, and place it on the table in front of you. You have come full circle; the exercise is complete. Slowly, gently, emerge back out through the layers of the orange, and relax for a minute or so. When you reopen your eyes, you should find that your vision is clearer and your mental faculties are more alert.

This exercise has been used for thousands of years to train people in the art of concentration. If you will practice this exercise every day for three weeks, once in the morning and again in the evening, you will develop the ability of fine-pointed concentration. You may go through some discouragement as you realize how little concentration you actually have. Do not give up, though, because that experience means you are about to break through the barrier of the old, undisciplined mind. The mind is like a muscle – the more you flex and train it, the more able it is to move how and where you want it to move. With faithful application, this exercise will enable you to become very adept at the art of concentration. The rewards, both physically and spiritually, will be plentiful.

In our Western culture, the intellect has become a god. We worship its development, training children from pre-school on to make it the central focus of life. Parents and school systems encourage and support vast amounts of mental activity in children, often excluding more important aspects of physical and emotional development. Our minds have been given a false sense of importance which borders on domination of our personality. In the experience of most people, the intellect has been developed so well through the educational process that our thinking is years beyond our emotional and spiritual development. This experience is common and unfortunate, because it puts us out of balance, making us lean too heavily on only one small part of our nature. OUR MINDS ARE NOT GOD.

Most people identify with their thoughts and mental ability as much as they do their bodies, seeing themselves as both body and mind. In order to experience a higher reality, it is necessary to break through this limited way of thinking. You are not your body, or your mind, or the products of your mind. That inner chatter that you hear when you first get up in the morning, the narrator who resides up in the frontal lobe, is not the real you. The real you inspires your mind with thoughts that reflect your true nature – which is like God. The mind thinks through the brain, which in turn instructs the body. In reality, the progression of influence moves in this order – from God through the soul, to the mind, through the brain, and finally, to the body.

There is a mental medium which is always operating throughout creation. It infuses the substance of the universe and is the way in which God functions throughout God's creation. This mental medium is the mind of Christ. This mind of God, or the Christ, makes it possible for all of us to communicate with each other and with the God who

74

fashioned it all. Most people think of their minds as their personal property. They think that, if original thoughts come into their minds, they own their thoughts as personal possessions. Some even think that their thoughts are private and off-limits to other people. In actuality, there are no original thoughts, because all existed in the mind of God eons before we ever glimpsed them.

Anyone who has a little sensitivity to other people can pick up on your thinking and very accurately understand it. Your mind is not a private compound with guard dogs and electronic surveillance set up to keep trespassers out. There is no such thing as your mind, my mind, his mind, or her mind. These are contrivances of the human ego which separate people from each other and from God. In reality, there is but One Mind, and we all use a portion of it. We use the mind of Christ in everything, and without it, no thoughts would pass and nothing could be accomplished.

The mind of Christ is the mind of God. When Jesus was on earth, he was a pure vehicle for the mind of God. "Christ" was not Jesus' last name – it means literally the anointed of God and signifies the power of God which was manifested in and through Jesus. Jesus was consciously at one with the Christ mind, and this "at-onement" enabled him to perform the works of teaching, redemption, and healing. Through his unity with God as a human being, he was able to bring humanity into atonement, or reconciliation, with its Creator.

The mind of God makes it possible for us to think into God's mind. Likewise, it allows God to think through ours. God created this mind in a way that makes all thoughts interconnected. As thoughts are emitted into the mind of God, they are acted upon in a way determined by the Laws inherent in God's being. Built into the Law of God is responsiveness to the thinking of God's creation. Our mind is not our possession; we just have use of it for a while.

There is only one mind. Anything that can ever be thought has already been thought.

The great artists and composers have realized that their ideas were given to them through divine revelation or inspiration. These musicians and poets have captured the music of the spheres, and the great inventors of all time are recombining already existent principles and extending them in the material realm. The one central medium through which these creative individuals receive these inspirations is the mind of Christ. We are not so powerful nor so independent that we of ourselves can do anything outside of the mind of God. Even Jesus said, "I, of myself, can do nothing." In other words, it is the power inherent in the mind of God which enabled Jesus to know what to do and have the ability to do it. God is the preexistent beginning, the process, and the end.

There is an old saying that there is nothing new under the sun. It is humbling to realize that we are not so special that we can come up with anything new in the way of ideas. We can develop better scientific processes and better this and that, but the ideas were there already in the mind of Christ. We simply have to get into position to receive them. Everyone has the use of the mind of God. All information is available to us, and all knowledge is possible for us to understand, if we get our own limited thinking out of the way enough. God's mind is present in and through everything, and it is active on all levels of creation – both seen and unseen.

When we communicate with another person, our words clothe our thoughts, and we express them. If there was not the fluid transferring medium of the mind of God through which to allow passage of these thoughts without distortion, we would not be able to understand each other. All attempts at communicating would be chaotic and random, and rarely would we be received properly. Every action is preceded by a thought which comes out of our use of the mind of God. The universe was created in the same way – by God holding a thought within God's mind and creating with God's Word: "Let there be Light."

In this same way, we can imitate God. Our thoughts are spoken silently within us first, and then they are projected outwardly where they will reap a physical effect. You are transmitting thoughts all the time. To predict your future, look at the thoughts that have been going through your mind, for this is what you will experience. If your thinking is gloomy or depressing, then your days ahead are likely to be gloomy or depressing. If your thinking radiates good will and beauty and joy, then your life will reflect these attitudes. We reap the fruits of our thoughts. What you think will become manifest.

For as people think in their hearts, so are they.
Proverbs 23:7

Every thought sets into motion the fulfillment of your desire, and your mind sees it already done. We become what we think. Even our environment is an expression of our thoughts. Because we are free in our use of the mind, it is difficult to stop our flow of thoughts. Mentally, we are completely free to transmit whatever we want. This is why we tend to get lazy in our thinking and just drift, letting our attention flit from flower to flower at random. Most of the time, we dwell on the results of past thinking, instead of cultivating more positive thoughts in order to make our future more in harmony with God.

The untrained mind rebels against discipline. If left untrained, it will jealously rule over your life, criticizing and judging, viewing life through a limited, negative filter. It indulges itself in whatever it wants, like a spoiled, intractable child. And, like a spoiled child, it will resist your initial attempts to regain control. Firm, consistent work will be necessary to retrain your mind. Your mind thinks it is in charge. But there is a part of you that is the real you and is truly in charge, one which uses your mind as a tool to create. This part some have called "soul." Your mind does not want to give up the throne it was allowed to usurp. Thus, the message must be firmly impressed upon your mind, by the power of your will and by the power of God, that it is not the ruler of your life. It is not God. You must train it to control itself, so that it is able to screen out all else but that which you want to concentrate upon. Your mind loves to be right, to inform you of things, to have all the answers. The seductive thing about the mind is that it is right at least half of the time, so it is difficult to totally discount it.

The soul uses the mind to create through the apparatus of your brain. Brain and mind are two distinctly different things. Your brain is the organic instrument through which your mind thinks. It is the receiving station which is inactive when you are sleeping. During sleep, the mind continues to operate the autonomic functions of the body through the sympathetic nervous system, while the brain channels the autonomic impulses. Mind exists beyond the use of the body.

If you have ever spent time with someone who is mentally handicapped, you might have sensed that there is something going on inside of him or her, that there is seemingly a person locked within an organism that does not function well. In truth, the individual is complete on the inside but cannot communicate effectively on the outside. There is a lot going on inside him or her, but the organic brain will not allow the mind to express fully, and you get the feeling that this person really has some deep experiences and insights about life, if only the organic vehicle would allow the expression to come through.

There was a story in the paper the other day which related the healing of a man from cancer by the use of laughter. This man apparently laughed himself well and overcame his prognosis of a few months to live. His mind made a decision, and his brain and body responded. There are lots of cases like this where the mind is used to overcome a physical disease. Some cancer clinics have their patients visualize small armies of cells coming in to devour the little cancer cells. They have been very successful. It should not surprise us that the mind can produce what it wants and that it has power over the flesh of our bodies. Mind is the creative agency in life. Whether you use this creative power positively or negatively is the major concern.

A number of years ago, I had an employee, an emotionally awkward young man in his twenties. About a month after he started working for me, he became concerned with a lump which had developed in his throat. He went to his doctor and was diagnosed as having cancer of the thyroid. He came in to work one afternoon very distressed, anticipating surgery within a couple of weeks. I pulled him aside and privately asked him what was going on in his life. I explained to him that illness was often the result of incorrect thinking or the response to a traumatic event in our life. The young man had never considered the possibility that something in his life could be causing the cancer and was surprised that I was giving him the responsibility to find out. After a few days, he shared with me the core problem. About three months before, he had met his first real girlfriend. He liked the young woman a lot, and they had started a fairly serious relationship.

A few weeks later, his brother, who was much more socially experienced, came home from college, and the girl became interested in his brother. His brother did not hesitate to take advantage of the situation, and so the young man lost the only girlfriend he had ever had to his more successful brother. He shared with me that he had never once discussed any of this with his brother, nor with anyone else. All of the anger and hurt and disappointment he had been feeling had been, quite literally, swallowed. I suggested to him that he confront his brother and express some of his pent-up feelings. Although it took him a few days to gather the courage to write his brother and explain his hurt and anger, he did it. He was in tears when he told me that he had taken the first step in releasing these feelings of loneliness and pain.

The mind creates, our bodies respond. The process is that simple. What is not so simple is to learn from our mistakes and begin to create what we really want. Most people are not even aware of the responsibility they were given when they were formed in the mind of Christ. People see very little connection between their experiences and the thoughts they have been thinking. Illness is not something that we experience at random, any more than happiness or success are. To say these happenings are random is to disregard the order inherent in the mind of Christ and to deny its power and reality.

In this young man's case, the week following his letter to his brother, when the pre-op check was performed, his diagnosis was changed from malignant to benign. A few weeks later, when he was operated on, they found a small, pea-sized tumor which, to my knowledge, did not have a recurrence of cancer. More importantly, he had learned that his thinking could influence his health. It was a valuable and enlightening experience for both of us.

I beseech you therefore, brothers, by the mercies of God, that you present your bodies as a living sacrifice, holy and acceptable to God... And be not conformed to this world, but be transformed by the renewing of your mind, that you may

prove what is that good, and acceptable, and perfect will of God.
Romans 12:1-2

The important issue is knowing how to be in accord with the mind of Christ. How do we put it on, as St. Paul exhorts us? What does this mean? The mind of Christ is the blueprint of how to be, how to create, how to function in this universe. It is fashioned perfectly. It always responds to our thinking and, through its immutable Law, it will give back to us whatever we think into it. Sometimes the responses come back to us immediately, sometimes after a while. All is dependent upon how strong our thinking is and how quickly we desire to learn from our mistakes.

This Law of Mind is set up to show us how to be. It is the great teacher; it instructs us through the experience of trial and error when we do not listen to the words of the prophets and saints. This Law returns to us every action, word, or thought we have placed into the mind of Christ – with a speed and power equal proportionally to the potency with which we have expressed those actions, words, thoughts. We get back what we put out. Whatever we are experiencing now is the result of our past thinking, acting, and speaking. Nothing that we can experience is possible without our making room for it through our thinking and actions.

If we want to develop some quality in our lives, we have to start creating it, by thinking and acting in harmony with what we want. If you want a friend, you have to start by being a friend to someone. If you want success, you have to remove thoughts of fear about failing and start thinking successful thoughts. Visualize yourself as a success. As you put on this mind of success, you are letting God know that you are really willing to become what you desire. You have to step out on your use of the mind of Christ by assuming

81

you already are and already have what you want. Then it will be given unto you.

The mind can be likened to a gardener in a fertile field. The gardener is the conscious, decisive aspect of our thinking; the fertile soil is like the subconscious part. When we make a decision or a prayer, it is like placing a seed into the fertile soil of the subconscious, where it begins to sprout and grow. The seed needs plenty of attention to develop into a mature plant, so the conscious gardener nourishes the seed with affirmations and keeps the field free from entangling fears and doubts. When it is mature, the seed – the prayer – will be harvested.

We cast thousands of seeds every day into the fertility of our subconscious mind. These seeds are at various stages of development and of a variety of types. When we allow ourselves to dwell on negativity, we can actually tear up the whole field – the good seeds as well as the ones we do not want. This usually happens when we see a large portion of our subconscious field loaded with weeds and useless plants. When we see this, we get upset, discouraged, depressed. This depression causes us to ignore the whole affair – to go to sleep or find some form of amusement to escape this dilemma.

To determine the usefulness of a plant is really not possible until it has matured to a certain point. If you have ever looked at a new sprout in a garden, you know what I mean. In the early stages of growth, it is difficult to tell whether that new sprout is a tomato, a cucumber, or a weed. So once the thought is planted, you have to wait a bit before you know what kind of plant it is. When the plant is ready, the subconscious always presents the seedling to the conscious mind for scrutiny. Then we have to decide whether we want to keep the plant in our garden. If we keep it and it grows, we can then harvest it and use it in our life. Every prayer works the same way. You throw the thought out like a seed, you let it grow, and then it is yours.

The trouble often emerges during harvest time. We are usually horrified at all of the rows and rows of useless plants which have cropped up in our mental garden – the careless thoughts and words, the meaningless actions, the wasted dreams and fantasies. These thoughts take up energy and space in our mental garden, space which could be used for more productive creations. Sometimes we feel so dismayed when we see this that we recoil in fear and ignore the whole garden. We do not want to take responsibility for those negative weeds which have our names written on the very fruit. Doing so would be too much to deal with, we feel, and we see the harvest approaching too soon to take any reparative action.

Unless you can confront these negative thoughts and uproot them, you are virtually stuffing plants back into the soil of the subconscious to grow and spread. At the next harvest, the plant will have grown larger and stronger, and this undesirable little plant may become a major problem in your life. It may send out poisonous runners to some of the better plants that are growing in your garden and be dangerously close to choking off the best plants you have been developing. In some cases, that one undesirable plant can even destroy the whole garden.

When harvest comes again for that weed plant, we are even more horrified at how overwhelming it is. Sometimes we despair at this point. This is the time to take action. The plant you have placed there by your thinking has to be dealt with, or you will not be able to go on. Sometimes it takes a good dose of courage to overcome the effects of your past negative thinking. Sometimes it takes talking to somebody who can be more objective about the nature of that plant. Remember, at the time of planting, you made the best decision you knew how to make, even if it was not ultimately the most constructive way of handling the situation.

If you are walking through a jungle in India and you hear the roar of a large Bengal tiger, you tremble with fear. The fear comes from the fact that you do not see it and you do not know exactly where it is. In the tall grasses, it could be stalking you, and you do not know from which direction it will lunge. It might bite you. The tiger who is not seen can cause more fear than a tiger who is standing right in front of you about to attack. This one you must look square in the face and decide whether to run or to fight. In this exchange, your imagination cannot run wild. Your enlarged image of the tiger diminishes somewhat when you confront it head-on. The problem is now manageable. The same is true of problem plants or qualities you have developed in your personal subconscious garden.

The key to getting away from having to confront negative thinking in the future is to clarify what you really want developed and brought to fruition. It is easy to blame others for our problems. We blame life, good and bad luck, our neighbors, and God for the situations in which we find ourselves. But if we are careful observers, we will be able to trace back from each event the means and process by which it was created, and then we can take full responsibility for our own actions. We will see the cause in our thinking which set that experience into motion.

We can have whatever we want. Thoughts of peace, giving, success, joy, love, and relatedness bring us health in mind and body. Thoughts of anger, resentment, domination, doubt, hatred, fear, and confusion bring illness and emotional imbalance. We get back from the mind of Christ what we put into it. There is no way out of that. That is the way we are made, the way we grow. Without this fail-safe, cause and effect Law, life would be chaotic, and experiences we have would be random. Then life would have the potential to be quite discouraging.

We have all been with people who make us feel drained and tired. Just being with them is painful, like the wind has been taken right out of our sails. Life seems meaningless and hopeless, and gloom and despair seem to follow them in everything they do. When you feel this way, it is because you have encountered the negative energy of these other people, and you have picked up on their emotional and mental atmosphere. Energy they are creating with their thinking makes you feel sick when you are with them. These people's hopelessness and listlessness is so strong that it affects you physically. You could react by trying to get away from them as quickly as possible. Or you could look more deeply and have compassion for the state in which they are living. It is their own thinking which produces these mental clouds and causes them to feel helpless. We can tune into their thinking and experience because of the interconnectedness of our minds in the mind of God. This connection we have with others is existent because there is only one mind which everyone is using.

The mind of Christ is so balanced and clear that no negativity can reside in accord with it. We use this Mind all the time, and we can benefit from its power to create. But we do not have to create with its balance and clarity. We are also free to miscreate with it. While our miscreations do not stain the mind of Christ in any way, they do affect us and those around us. If we want to avoid these miscreations, we can be in accord with the mind of Christ by seeking to familiarize ourselves with it. This takes work, no question about it. All the habits of our dark thinking are very difficult to change.

We see this difficulty of change in any of our efforts to improve our bodies or minds. Our body wants to keep its habits, and we do not want to make the effort to fight our body's rebellion when it cannot have its way anymore. So we just give in and let it rule us. Habits of thinking are harder to change than habits of the body. They are like grooves in a record that has been played over and over. These grooves almost attract the stylus because of how many times the same track has been grooved out. Thinking is just like this. Thinking is not easy to change. Yet, thinking is the first thing you must change if you want to change yourself.

A wise man once told me that I had to put my mind at the top of the ladder if I ever wanted my feet to follow. Put in your mind an image of how you want to be, and affirm deliberately that you are becoming that. Keep out all thinking that denies this new you. Assume that you can become what you want to become, and then act in accordance with your prayer. This is not just wishful thinking, because you are using the mind of Christ to help you become what you want to be.

The mind of Christ is creative – it nourishes and builds things up. It supports all living things. It does not condemn anyone. It does not hold grudges. It does not think more highly of itself than of other people. It keeps concentrated on the work at hand. It puts 100% effort into producing the desired result. It does not tire. It does not get sick or diseased. It is always at peace and filled with light and life. Suffering and pain are not an experience within the mind of Christ. But yet, suffering and pain seem to be the only way we finally break through to become one with the mind of Christ. Whenever we break an old pattern of thinking, there is a little pain and suffering. Whenever we love more than we are used to love being given to us, we experience a little pain. If love and giving are muscles that we seldom use, and then we start using them, they get stretched and strengthened by the exercise. This produces discomfort and pain. But like physical exercise, it is a good pain, because you know you are getting results.

Experiencing the mind of Christ is not a one-time happening, any more than the baby looking at the mother for the first time is satisfied with one look. The baby must look and look, and it remains in awe for months and years. So too, tasting of the mind of Christ will establish you as a baby in relation to God, because it is awesome and wonderful and overwhelming. It is much bigger than we are, but it is so beautiful that we will want to bond like a baby bonds with its mother. We will feel we are coming home when we experience it.

This mind of Christ will begin to inspire you with compassion and understanding. It might possibly awaken you to some of the things you know you should be doing but have not yet. It will communicate to you, after some time, and tell you things that you need to know. If we can talk to It, then It can talk to us. This is the whole process of meditation. Meditation is listening to God.

To experience the mind of Christ, it is necessary to let your desire be known to God. Tell God what you want; tell God that you want to experience the mind of Christ. Then get very quiet, and release all the thinking you are working on at the moment. Give yourself over to this mind, and let It fill you with Itself. Hold this experience inside of you for a few minutes, and then go about your affairs. Do this two times a day for about ten minutes a sitting. If you do not get results the first time, just keep it up, because you are making a new pattern. Creating a new pattern usually takes three to seven repetitions, in order for it to be solidified. Put yourself on the line for this experience. Make room for this experience by organizing your time so that you have ten minutes in the morning and ten minutes at night. Your body will get the idea that you are serious about this, and it will accommodate your desire to have the experience of the mind of Christ.

To meditate, still your thinking, and be quiet inside. Let go of all thoughts and concerns of the day, and let your desires lift and fly away. Talk to God, and tell God that you are doing this to be closer to God. Tell God you want God to guide and direct your meditation. Give your mind over to God to inspire it and fill it with God's Self. Then, sit and let all thinking flow freshly, not narrating your thoughts or resisting anything. You will know when you feel God's presence or hear God's voice. It will not be so strange that you will not be able to consciously know it is God. God's guidance will be fresh and clear. Gradually, you will become more able to easily connect with the mind of God and to hear God's voice speaking to you. Meditation is a creative, receptive process which takes a lifetime to master.

ξ

CHAPTER FIVE

WORD

In the beginning was the Word. And the Word was with God.
And the Word was God.
John 1:1

Several years ago, I made a pilgrimage to the Boston area to meet a certain priest. Some friends had told me I would benefit from meeting him, as he had a deep understanding of the spiritual life. When I arrived at his house, it was late at night, so I decided to wait until the next morning to introduce myself. That night, I had a very powerful dream. In the dream, I was with a man who was unknown to me but with whom I felt very comfortable. He was giving me instruction, explaining something of great interest, when all at once, some thugs came toward us carrying clubs, chains, and knives. The man placed me behind him and, at once, we were both within a small white picket fence enclosure with a short closed gate. The fence could easily have been jumped by a medium-sized child. He stood sideways to the gang of thugs and told me to be still and watch.

As the gang approached, he said the word "No" very consciously and firmly. Again he repeated it, all the while never wavering in his attention to the approaching danger. Seven times, he said the word "NO!," and one by one each thug dropped his weapon and dispersed.

This man knew that his decision was going to be obeyed; there seemed to be no doubt in his mind. I was humbled by this experience, which was as real and as vivid as if you were leaning against me right now and I could feel the weight of your physical presence. The dream impressed me so deeply that I woke up and pondered it for a time. Then, I went back to sleep and seemingly forgot about it.

In the morning, I went to meet the priest we had come to see. When I was brought in to see him, I was stunned to see that he was the man from my dream. I did not ask him if he knew about what he had shown me that night, but, being naive at the time, I was certain he was absolutely conscious of the experience. Later, I realized it did not matter if he was conscious of it or not. He had taught me a very important lesson. He taught me the power of the Word. I learned that what I say will happen when I know that it will. The Word can bring life or destroy it, depending on how it is used.

When God imagined this universe, God held it in concentrated attention. When God felt it was time, God breathed forth the Word, causing the successive chains of cause and effect to manifest. This Word carried all of the vibratory rates of frequency and possibility which still reverberate today and will continue forever. God's Word is still creating from the original Word God spoke. Through the creative potency of the Word, God brought all the worlds and galaxies, seen and unseen, into being. God placed this same Word within the core of each human being, and it is this original potential and possibility which we use on a microcosmic scale when we create through our word.

We have all been engaged in a conversation in which someone we are talking to emphatically states that a certain thing is so. There is a conviction in his statement that seems rock-solid, with no doubts. This individual is using the power of the Word and what he affirms will be so for him. Likewise, when we really do not want something or do not agree with something, we have the power to negate. These are decisions upon which we put our "word." This "word" that we speak, whether silently or verbally, is what determines how the power of God moves through us and what experiences will take place in our lives. When we say "yes" to something, we are actually creating a space through which it can manifest; when we say "no" to something we are actually sealing ourselves off so that it will not become a part of our experience. The more conscious we are of this creative power, the more potency will be in our thoughts, words and prayers.

And they were all amazed and spoke among themselves, saying, "What a word is this!" For with authority and power he commanded the unclean spirits, and they came out..

Luke 4:36

Each of us uses the Word each day to create our own reality. Through the creative potency of the Word, we exert authority over the affairs of our lives. As we come to know the Will of God through hearing God's Word within us, we will have influence over a wider sphere. Jesus Christ demonstrated this authority in everything he did. He did nothing of his own will. Instead, he listened to the Father and followed what he was instructed to do. Because he was perfectly obedient to the will of God, his every action carried the unobstructed power and majesty of the living Word.

It is through God's prophets and servants that we are shown the gifts which mankind has been given. Each messenger was sent by God to perform a particular mission – some for the whole world, and some for a given people. The greatest of these instruments of God were the ones whose word became flesh. And of those, none is greater than Jesus Christ. What he said took place. Jesus was the clearest channel for God that has ever set foot on earth. His will was simply and purely to do God's will. In this, he was the Word made flesh, and he embodied this totality from his baptism to his ascension. Every action in his life demonstrated how we are to use our God-given right to create. Only through knowing God's will for us can we create in harmony with God.

That is where the work comes in. It takes plenty of "pick and shovel" work to become open enough to allow the mind of God to overshadow our minds and thereby reveal God's will for us. Remember, God will not force us. We must volunteer for this, as spiritual seekers have done through the ages. The best way to condition yourself to be open to the will of God is to read the scriptures and the lives of holy people. Read the accounts of people who gave their lives in love for other people, for these people come the closest to being like God. It is their example that we must follow if we are going to experience what it is like to hear God's Word in us. God's Word brings life and freedom; human words bring darkness and limitation.

In the desert after his baptism, Jesus was tempted by the devil to turn stones into bread. This was a strong temptation, because Jesus had been fasting for perhaps three or four weeks, and we can assume he was in a weakened condition. His humanity was sorely tested during this time. He was subject to the same concerns as we are – the same feelings and emotions, the same physical yearnings. Jesus was just like us in that he was tempted as we are; however, he was different in that he overcame his temptations. His response to temptation is our example, showing us how to overcome our own temptations. Jesus said, "It is written, man shall not live by bread alone, but by every Word that proceeds out of the mouth of God" (Matthew 4:4).

What does this mean? How can words be food? Consider that, within the Word of God, all rates of vibratory frequency exist. God is present in all atoms, molecules, and light particles. This means that God is the source of our material supply. When we want things for ourselves and try to supply them without acknowledging God, we demonstrate very little trust in God. Jesus trusted God so completely that he depended entirely upon God for both material and spiritual sustenance. He did eat food, but it was when God moved him to eat, not when his desires were driving him to eat. He refused to eat when the world said he should be hungry as a demonstration of his total reliance on God.

God's Word is life and health for us. If we could train ourselves to listen to it and obey it, we would be at peace and life would become meaningful again. The word "obey" often conjures up feelings of being forced, that we "have to" do something. The connotation is similar to the word "discipline;" often people cringe when they see it in print or hear it. But what we neglect to realize is that these two words have often been misunderstood because of human error. The word "obey" comes from the root *audire*, which means "to perceive or hear." The word "discipline" means "training," that which is designed to produce a pattern of behavior. These are not coercive, punitive concepts, but instead they are practices which are essential to spiritual growth and development.

Without training and openness to new perceptions, we cannot grow. It is essential for us to change many things as we go through life, because we will outgrow the old ways and the new ways will provide a means for greater expansion. When we train ourselves to receive God's Word, we then have to follow it and live it out in action. This takes discipline and obedience. Love is also necessary. Obedience without love is really not obedience – it is slavery. Slavery, by its very nature, implies resentment and fear of punishment. Fear is the opposite of love, and it is the worst motivator of which I know. Fear will always kick back on you at some point. When the thing you have been fearing disappears, your motivation dissolves. If you are doing something because you have to and not out of love, it will fail over time.

To train yourself to hear God's Word within you, it is necessary to get yourself to the point where you want to hear God more than you want anything else. In my early twenties, I had an experience which brought me the realization of this truth. At that time in my life, I felt a pressing need to know what I was supposed to be doing here on earth, if not in some cosmic sense, then at least in a mundane sense. I had become dissatisfied with the type of work I had been doing and felt the need for a new direction in life. I began to apply myself to this question of purpose and made a prayer for some guidance. Within a short time, I managed to become quite frustrated, with no direction in sight.

During this time, I attended a retreat and discussed my quandary with my spiritual director. My director advised me to meditate on God's will for my life and sent me off to the chapel. For three grueling days, I cycled through rounds of asking and listening and asking and listening, hoping for any answer from God. I would get quiet and set up my question very carefully, make contact with God within the center of my being, ask the question, and then sit, wait, and be open. I did this for 20 minutes at each sitting, eight times a day for two whole days, with no results. By nightfall on the third day, I was very discouraged and began to feel a pervading sense of failure. I realized that it was time to let it go or give up. At bedtime, I asked once more in one final, valiant "give it up to God" finale. It was then that I heard the words: "Go back to school."

Upon hearing that guidance, I was shocked and appalled and surprised and excited, all at the same time. It was very clear to me that this was correct guidance, even though my mind did not like the idea of going back to school. Many years before, I had crossed off the educational process as a waste of time; but since I had God on the line, I asked some other pressing questions – like "Why?" for instance. God told me that it was important to have the credibility in the eyes of the world, which the degree would provide. Then I asked what I should study, and I heard the word "psychology." This answer brought me no small amount of discomfort, as I did not think very highly of the field, and so I was beginning at this point to experience some resistance to the guidance I was receiving.

The final surprise came when I asked how I was to support my family and go to school at the same time. God told me to open a restaurant with my wife. Despite the turbulence I was experiencing mentally, there was a deeper part of me that resonated with all this. The deeper part knew that what I had heard was true and real and of God. As I processed what I had been told, it all started to make sense, and I stepped out in the faith that I had a God-given direction.

It was the clearest inner guidance I had received up to that point, and the process of receiving it opened up my entire being. God actually spoke to me, and that realization affected me profoundly. The fruits of this process confirmed that I was not alone and that I was cared for. Now I knew that God was concerned about me – not just in a general, objective way, but in a way that was deeply personal and intimate. Within God's guidance for me, I recognized the mark of a loving Father and knew intuitively that what God had given me was exactly what I needed. It was not like God was handing me something on a gold platter; following God's direction was going to take work and time and money and effort. But I was clear about the direction in which I was to go and certain that it was exactly what I should do.

Within ten weeks, I had built the restaurant with the help of some friends, and I had enrolled at the University. What had started in late September was already rolling at the end of December that same year. At once, I had an income, I had the business, and I had started school, just by getting my thinking out of the way long enough to hear God's Word for me.

Since that point, I have applied the same principles to important matters in my life, especially matters relating to other people and my interactions with them. What has impressed me about this process of receiving guidance from God and listening to God's direction is that it very rarely conforms to what I want personally. It is almost always a relief to receive an answer, because it is what you or others really need and not merely what is being demanded. The clarity of God's voice is a refreshing respite from the confused desires and thoughts of our short-sighted humanity.

People want a lot of things which are absolutely no good for them. But people have a right to these useless things, whether they be personality affectations or material things. Usually it is the case that, when people are so adamant about what they want, they never stop and ask themselves if their characters will be perfected by such acquisitions. Or are they merely covering over with these possessions the better part of their divinity in the process? Obtaining what we want, without getting direction on whether it is best for us, will often result in pain and suffering. This is why it is very important to develop a certainty of contact with God, so that you are sure you have God's attention when you speak to God.

In seeking this certainty, you will feel God's presence overshadow you, and you will know that God is there loving and guiding you. When you have this feeling, then you can ask God your questions and tell God your needs, and God will respond. If you keep your ideas and opinions and desires out of the process, God will not have to compete with your thinking. God's voice will become clearer and clearer as you build this bond and practice being inwardly still. This voice is not selfish, it is not boastful, it is not angry or jealous. It is not concerned with pettiness or malice. It is safe, whole, loving, and wise. You will know It when you hear It, and there will be no doubt as to Its origin. The

Soundless Voice will be heard, and when you hear it, you will know that, on a deeper level, you have always known that Voice.

The Word of God can come through anyone regardless of their development, if they get their thinking out of the way. If we truly want to hear what God has to say about what we want to know, then we will be open enough to let the answer come to us. As we open, we can clear our likes and dislikes away and let God give us God's guidance for the situation. This is what Jesus meant when he told the devil that we are to "live by every word that proceeds from the mouth of God." To live as Jesus teaches us to live is so fulfilling that all of our desires will be satisfied, and our thirst will be quenched. Knowing God's will for us in a given situation makes us certain, and this certainty brings us peace. Doubt and fear disappear in the face of such certainty.

I think it is no less a virtue to know how to remain silent well than to know how to speak well. And it seems to me that men should have a neck like a crane's, so that their words would go through many joints before they came out of the mouth.
- The Sayings of the Brother Giles

The tongue is the rudder of the whole ship. If it wags relentlessly and drivels out slander and gossip, then the result of our words will be confusion and negative experiences slung back at us. This occurs very precisely through the Law of cause and effect. The tongue can only speak what is in the heart....for out of the abundance of the heart the mouth speaks.
Matthew 12:34

But I say to you, that every idle word that men shall speak, they shall give account thereof in the day of judgment.
Matthew 12:36

For by your words you shall be justified, and by your words you shall be condemned.
Matthew 12:37

If any man among you seems to be religious, and bridles not his tongue, but deceives his own heart, this man's religion is vain.
John 1:26

Our speech is so important, because we are expressing through our words the things we desire. The heart has desires which produce thoughts, and the mind thinks these thoughts which are unspoken words; eventually these thoughts come through the lips as words, to produce what we will later experience. God's Word within us is without hatred, slander, or prejudice. It is always creative and positive. It always blesses and uplifts. It never condemns. We condemn ourselves by the misuse of our words.

Jesus was the first to become so clear a channel for God's Word that there was no resistance at all to the will of God. He sacrificed his human will to allow the Divine Word to flow so completely through him that he alone could say he was One with God. All the actions and words of Jesus were God's Word, complete and whole. Being in this way is possible for every person, if each one completely sets the human will aside. This involves loving God so much that you want to be with God always in your thinking and actions. In this way, you love God so fully that you ask God before you act, before you speak, and before you set anything into motion. This love will form the bridge which will enable you to uncover the Word of God residing in you. It will give you new ears and new eyes. Your ship will finally have a reliable navigator.

It is God's will for us to become one with God. Jesus has told us, "These things which I do, so shall ye do and even greater things still." With these words, Jesus is saying, "I did it, and so you can do it too." But our doing so takes disciplining our words and our thoughts, so that we can get simple enough to understand what God is telling us.

A few years back, I was given an exercise which required me to remove from my speech for one week the use of the words "I," "me," or "my." At first, the exercise seemed simple enough, but in actuality, it was a very difficult task. I had to say things like, "That is very tasty," or, "Today is really beautiful." It was not allowable to refer to myself in any way, and I would catch myself rebelling and slipping up with the exercise. But what this exercise taught me was that we are so completely self-absorbed that we rarely look at life from another perspective besides our own. What does God think of today? How does God view the situations in our lives? What is going on inside of other people? We cannot truly know the answer to these questions until we are willing to sacrifice our own opinions and judgments. This exercise opens us up to much less personal attachment to the affairs of our lives. It helps us begin to see from God's perspective. We need to get simple and stop feeling that our thoughts and ideas are so important.

Let your words be kind, helpful, truthful, and necessary. Give no place in your mental cabinet for the storage of resentment or grudges. Use your thinking to create words that bless, that heal and bring peace to troubled hearts. Speaking only what is necessary or kind builds interest in your spiritual storehouse. It is difficult at first to change the mental habits of putting people and things down, but with a little effort, your silent words will be helping you overcome your own separation from God. As you start to think the way you suspect God thinks, it will be easier for you to hear God tell you directly what God sees. All of the major religions have scriptures which, if followed, will bring you closer to God. It is just a matter of doing what they say.

And he was clothed in a vesture dipped in blood; and his name is called The Word of God.
Revelations 19:13

For the Word of God is alive and active. It cuts more keenly than any two-edged sword, piercing as far as the place where life and spirit, joints and marrow, divide. It sifts the purpose and thoughts of the heart.
Hebrews 4:12

A clear mind, one that is free from negation and unconscious patterns of judgment, is necessary if you are going to develop a relationship with the living God. Here is an exercise to help you change the mental pattern of criticism and judgment. Try this for the next seven days: when you drive by someone or pass someone on the street, ask God to bless him with what he needs. See the person strong, happy, and vital. See him loved by his Creator and filled with peace. Ask God to do this for him. Do it quickly and then let go of this blessing. If you are not sure what kind of blessing to give the person, picture him experiencing some good which everyone could use in their lives, or turn it over to God to give that individual what he really needs. Through your blessings, you will begin to experience letting God's Word work through you. After a while, you will realize that as you are blessing this other person, you are being blessed as well. For a blessing heals both the receiver and the channel.

§

CHAPTER SIX
LIGHT

The light of the body is the eye; if, therefore, your eye be single, your whole body shall be full of light. But if your eye be evil, your whole body will be full of darkness. If, therefore, the light that is in you bedarkness, how great is that darkness!

Matthew 6:22-23

My first experience of seeing light occurred when I was nineteen years old. At nineteen, I was skeptical of the possibility that any human being could know God, or that any had any significant experience of God which was not merely hearsay or blind faith. Most of the spiritual works that I had read seemed to be just words coming from empty shells. I was feeling an intense calling to the spiritual life, but I had found no one whom I felt could instruct me.

At the time, I was working as an orderly in a hospital, and one of my co-workers was a young man who told me that he was a brother in a Christian order and was studying for the priesthood. I assumed he was a Catholic, since that was the only priesthood of which I was aware. But the young man told me that the order to which he belonged had no church affiliation. Sensing my interest, he invited me to come home with him sometime to meet his spiritual director. I politely declined, but I had a hard time putting our conversation out of my mind.

A few days later, my curiosity got the best of me, and I took him up on his offer. The young man took me to a large house located in a rather tough, run-down neighborhood. Inside, I was surprised to find clean, well-kept rooms, simple but comfortable. The walls were painted in a light color, and here and there hung pictures of saints, of Jesus, and of the Blessed Virgin. On a bookshelf in the parlor was a small frame which caught my eye. In careful, hand-done calligraphy were the words: "Your actions speak so loudly I can't hear a word you say." There was a faint smell of frankincense in the air and a sacred presence which heightened my senses.

Into this scene walked a man dressed in black clerical garb. The man appeared to be in his late twenties and was strong and very vibrant. He had a round, cheerful face and a look of clarity and knowing in his eyes. Needless to say, I was a bit taken aback, because he was not at all what I expected. What especially put me off was his traditional black suit and Roman collar. With characteristic directness, I asked him why he wore those funny clothes. He seemed amused by my question, but he answered me simply, "Because it gets the job done." His answer was so real that it took me a few minutes to digest it. We talked for about 40 minutes, as he answered my pressing questions about life, the spiritual journey, and a myriad of things. Before meeting this man, I had nearly concluded that nobody on earth had truly experienced or known God.

Because nobody seemed to truly know what they were talking about when they talked about God, I felt that the experience of God was relegated to the pages of antiquity and to the brave pioneers of the past. The saints yes, they had clearly had real experience and relationship with God, but the priests, nuns and other devout individuals of our time clearly did not have this experience. And yet here I was with this young priest who was surprisingly happy and who exuded a deep sense of peace. He answered each of my questions with adeptness and a knowing twinkle in his eye. As we conversed, I was beginning to feel like I was home for the first time in my life. Deep within me, I felt a sense of centeredness and assurance building. My doubts began to disappear, and I was running out of questions. At that point, I was left sitting across from his desk feeling both inspired and a little bewildered.

As I continued to look at him, my eyes began to lose their ability to focus. My peripheral vision closed down to a small focal point in the middle of my visual field. I saw waves of light pulsing out from the center of this man, moving in currents across the room and washing over me. The priest smiled with a knowing smile. When I told him I was having trouble seeing, he smiled even more broadly. The light kept coming in waves, and I felt a mild ecstasy come over me. I was certain at this point that I was in the right place and needed to learn from this man. Thus, for nine years, I was a student in this order, and everything this priest told me about God and the spiritual world eventually came to be my own personal experience.

The window of the soul is the eye, through which the light shines from the Self. If our hearts are filled with negative feelings and pain, then the eyes will be covered with that glaze of negativity and pain, and little light will pass from the soul/Self into the physical body. Light comes through the spiritual body into the physical one through the connecting points of sympathetic ganglia and the spinal column. There is some light in every person, or the body could not function. The degree of light in each human body depends on the soul's development and the condition of outer brain/body consciousness. Those who never acknowledge God in a heartfelt way have very little light shining out into the physical form. On the other hand, those consciously striving to love, know, and experience God directly develop an increase of light in and around the body.

The question we must ask ourselves in relation to the light is this: am I seeking the light for myself and my own aggrandizement, or am I seeking the light so that I might serve God better? If your answer implies only a selfish motive, then you will have to work on your character and self-discipline for a while before you set the other goal in mind. Building character involves doing things we might not like to do, such as cleaning the house, the bathroom, or doing dishes. Sometimes it involves going places to accomplish something specific, or serving people who need it most. Often, building character requires us to be inconvenienced to the point of frustration, until we wake up and realize that doing something for someone else without thought of ourselves is the surest path to spiritual growth.

If our whole attention is on God (or on our divinity), and our thinking is clear of negation, then our body will be full of light. There are forces acting within the soul which bring about instantaneous Illumination when we let go and let God. The New Testament records the Illumination of St. Paul as he traveled the road to Damascus. He was knocked off his horse and blinded by an incredible light, which filled his body and caused him to be led around like a child for three days. This is the reality of the Christ light, the light which comes from God shining in peace and power at the center of our being. Our eye is single when we place all our cares and concerns before God and look only to God's presence and light. Then our body will fill with a light so real and visible that we cannot deny its radiance. This light changes the very cells of our bodies and brings our thinking into harmony with God.

Until we have seen the Self within, we do not truly know ourselves. In order to see something, we must first have light by which to see. This light is not the "light of understanding" or the "light of knowledge," or the various other ways we may want to interpret it. Light is the emanation of the Life-force from the God-Self within. It is real. It is observable spiritually and physically, and it causes definite changes in the body when it increases.

It is an awe-filled thing to fall into the hands of the living God. But call to remembrance the former days, in which, after you were illuminated, you endured a great fight of afflictions.
Hebrews 10:32-33

I will never forget the day of my coming into the Illumination. I had spent the day fishing with a life-vowed brother from the order. The brother had offered to teach me to fish, with the implication that in so doing I would learn how to be a fisher of men. We arrived at the lake mid-morning. The air was still and warm, and I was full of expectation. I had fished a little as a boy, but I had never been very successful at it. We fished for hours, while the brother filled me with homespun fishing advice and spiritual metaphor. By the end of the day, I was doubly disappointed. The only thing I had caught all day was a small duck which had tangled its foot on my line. The brother also had caught nothing at all, and he had exhausted his storehouse of spiritual wisdom. We drove back to the brotherhouse in silence.

When we arrived, the house seemed deserted. We went into the parlor and turned on the television. After about twenty minutes, the house father came out of his office and joined us. Within a short time, I began to feel a fire come over my body. It happened quite suddenly, like an intense fever. My eyes began to have trouble focusing, and my head felt like it was pushing through the confines of my skull. Soon I looked over at the priest, who seemed to be watching me out of the corner of his eye, and I told him what I was experiencing. He looked at me deeply for a moment, and then he sent me up to the chapel with the instructions to spend some time kneeling in front of the shrine to the Blessed Mother. I did what I was told.

Upstairs in the chapel, I knelt in front of the shrine in fervent prayer. A fire of Light was coming over me in intense waves, and I was sweating profusely. I had the sense as I knelt there that my concepts, like dry chaff, were burning up in this fierce light and power. I knew that my mind was undergoing a personal death and was only vaguely aware of my surroundings. After a time, I was joined in the chapel by the brothers and sisters who had come in for evening prayers. Someone began to sing, and as I turned to face the altar, I was astounded to see the Lord Jesus standing before me. He was beautiful, enormous, and ablaze with light. His presence was so full that my body burned, and I lost consciousness and fell to the ground.

A well-meaning brother came over and helped me up to my knees. I was drenched with perspiration as I looked up at the figure still before me. His face was stern, but loving. As I gazed at him, the light around him began to increase to the point that I could no longer see anything but brilliant white light, brighter than the brightness of the sun. I felt an invisible crown of thorns being placed on my head and was certain that the beads of sweat pouring unto my shirt were blood from the prick of the thorns. Once again, I fell over unconscious. This time, I felt as though I had been pushed onto the carpet by an unseen hand, and I was certain that it was the humiliation I needed from the loving hand of my Lord. I felt his awesome authority and love purging and chastening me, until there was nothing left but him. Regaining consciousness again, I struggled back up to my knees, feeling ashamed of my former life and how far from God I had wandered.

Then, I became aware that the brothers and sisters had filed out of the chapel after finishing their prayers, and I was once more alone in the silence. The priest in charge came in, and the candles were lit on the altar. I was brought up to the altar, and the priest laid his hands on my head, saying some words of blessing. He asked for the light of Christ to be sealed in my body and made the sign of the cross. I felt completely absorbed in a radiant, glorious ecstasy. I slept that night in the chapel, close to the Master, feeling like a newly born infant – loved, protected, and reborn.

For four days afterward, I experienced a tremendous regeneration of my body. My thinking was more simple and childlike. I felt heaven infusing my flesh and my mind. By the fourth day, I still feltlightness in my body, but I was surprised and dismayed to discover that old patterns of thinking were beginning to infiltrate my mind. I began to wrestle with these imperfections I could see and began to be very troubled. Despite all I had been taught before my Illumination, I still harbored the expectation that this experience had wiped out all temptation and all possibility of error.

Now I found, on the contrary, that my errors were flooding up in my face, much like increased light in a room will illuminate all the blemishes and dirt. The dichotomy of being blessed with the Christ light and at the same time having many things to overcome and work on humbled me sufficiently, and I began to work and pray that these things be transformed. I remembered the scripture where St. Paul talks about the afflictions which follow the Illumination, and I knew that I was definitely in the throes of them.

When the light of Christ comes into our flesh, changes in attitude, thinking, and feeling occur. It is as if the very atoms within each cell were changing the tilt of their axis to point toward God. Formerly, the atoms in our body were polarized to the earth, but when the light of Christ enters, they become oriented to the mind of Christ. Our physical body takes on a new lightness of being, and our devotional work takes on greater depth and fervency. Taking on the light of Christ is both an event and a process. The process of coming into the Christ light takes work in letting go of things to which you have been clinging, things not of the light. Preparation for the light involves cleansing the body and mind of worldly thinking and purging our conscious minds of negative patterns. Great strength and resolution are necessary, since the first things we must confront are our errors and selfishness.

"Letting go" is a term which has been kicked around by many people to describe giving over to God. What is often overlooked, however, is the experience of letting go, which involves loosing our precious habits and opinions concerning life. Sometimes the process of letting go involves losing friends or severing other close relationships. Our attitudes and emotional reactions are transformed by the letting go process. This process can be very intense. It involves a complete re-evaluation of oneself and a recognition that we are nothing before God. There comes a point in this process when we realize that nothing we have accomplished by our own plans and efforts has been enduring. This is very humbling. We come to realize that nothing we devised ourselves has turned out well in the long run, and we are left examining a failed life without any real relationship to God. We often resist spending time on our knees, and we are uncomfortable with the feeling that without God we are nothing.

Things used to be so easy before we began our spiritual striving for God. At least, before we began to consciously desire oneness with God, life seemed fairly harmless and satisfying. We may look around at other peoples' seemingly placid lives and wonder why things seem so difficult for us. Do not be fooled by appearances. Other people may look happy, but they are never going to be truly at peace until they attain the light and have a direct, personal relationship with their Father. The first thing to do is to ask God to bring the light to you, and then to begin to fill your body and mind with it. Once you have done this, things will begin to shift in you.

Be forewarned: when we turn on a light in a dark room, it shows everything up, and the brighter the light, the greater the visible details. When the light begins to increase in us, everything that was comfortably placed in our personal room is now open for scrutiny. It is uncomfortable to have our opinions, grudges, fears, and selfishness exposed in the glaring light of Illumination. This is the type of scrutiny which occurs when we ask that the light enter our body and mind. It is not that the light by its nature is disturbing; rather, the fact that our life may be so out of accord with God that our whole life may need adjusting is the element that can be disturbing. Sometimes even our health is affected, while cells cleanse out the effects of years of negative thinking and bad habits.

Each magnificent experience on the spiritual path is a new beginning – by no means the perfected, final product. Once I had taken the step into being filled with light, I had to learn to function with it. The Illumination is an initiation, which means that something was begun in me. It not only made a tremendous change in my life, but it also required that I continue to change as a result. I was not given this experience because I was in some way "worthy." All spiritual initiation is the result of the unmerited Grace of God. We are given spiritual experience when, through our efforts, we have let go enough to let the Grace of God flow into us.

My son, despise not the chastening of the Lord, nor faint when you are rebuked by Him; for whom the Lord loves He chastens, and scourges every son whom He receives. If you endure chastening, God deals with you as sons; for what son is he whom the Father chastens not? But if you be without chastisement, whereof you are all partakers, then you are bastards, and not sons.
Hebrews 12:5-8

This light is real, and it will bring all parts of our life into harmony with God. We do not possess the light; it is of God and of Christ. When this light begins to build in our physical temple, we have developed to the point of accepting God's direction to some small degree in our lives. This light is God's nature, and the way the light functions is the way God functions. The light purifies and clears away misconceptions and disease. It will show up all things not in accord with its nature, and by its nature, it will transform them.

On our journey back home to God, the first step is longing for home. We imagine the peace and joy of being home with God, and our desire to experience this draws us closer to God. We begin to look to God to help us, knowing that the journey will be impossible through our own feeble efforts. As we look more and more to God through prayer and meditation, God draws closer to us and we to God. As we move closer, we begin to experience God's presence within and around us. The first thing we discern is light. We may perceive this light during a meditation as a subtle, milky glow emanating from within us, or we may actually glimpse it surrounding our physical body. This light is the evidence of God's presence increasing in our lives, and those who have eyes to see its presence will see it.

I am the light of the world; he that follows me shall not walk in darkness but shall have the light of life.
John 8:12

After a year and a half of work within this Christian order, I had the experience of having my whole body fill with the Light of Christ. Instead of merely seeing the light in and around others, I saw and felt it infuse the cells of my body and head. Now, when I shut my eyes and look inside my body, all I see is light. The circumstances preparing me for this experience are beyond the scope of this chapter. What is important to say about preparation for the light is this: we need a guide who has this experience and thus knows how to prepare us for it and show us the way. Often, God will guide us to some trustworthy soul who has the key to the next step of our spiritual journey home. Prayer, meditation, and study of scripture are the keys for developing a relationship with God. The light will gradually increase as it pulses forth from the Self and our outer being opens to receive it more and more. Letting the light into our being is natural and does not require any mental or emotional contortions. Remember, we of ourselves can do nothing. If we merely get ourselves out of the way, this light will automatically shine into our temples and illuminate us.

Now, I would like to pass on to you two exercises which I was given in preparation for the Illumination. Faithful practice of these exercises will help you to come closer to the light:

1. Make a prayer to God to guide your exercise and protect you from all harm and things contrary to God's nature. Clear your thinking and be still inside your heart. Look within your temple, to the center of your being, for the light. At first you may see only darkness, but the fact that you are looking brings eventual response from your soul. Do this every day for 15 minutes, morning and evening, for three weeks. If you see something inside of you that you do not like, ask God to take it away or change that condition in you. If something scares you, then do the same thing. At the end of each sitting, thank God for his help.

2. The next exercise involves sitting for 15 minutes a day, imagining a ball of light starting at your feet and moving up through your entire body. The ball of light must be seen as pure, white light and large enough to fit comfortably over your shoulders. First, spend time visualizing it until you see it very clearly. This is going to take concentration, as does everything which is meaningful. When you have this ball of light before you in the same intensity and shape as the sun in the sky, then place it at your feet. Slip your feet into it,

and bring the ball of light slowly up through the various parts of your body. Let the light soak in at each point, until you feel the change it brings. This light brings peace and regeneration, and it will sensitize your body, bringing each organ into balance and perfect working order. Do this exercise once a day for three weeks.

Work with one of these exercises at a time. It is important to learn to take instructions as they are given, in order to be able to be directed by God. We first learn obedience to our elders in order to one day be able to take guidance's directly from our Creator. If direction is given with love, then obedience is the natural response of our souls. Record your results in a daily spiritual journal, so that you can see the progress and the process. This is not an exotic, complicated practice. The writings of the saints and mystics are replete with many such experiences. These experiences are the natural result of a human being's serious, consistent striving to know and serve God. Seeing light in the body is necessary for good health. Seeing only darkness is the sickness which is so prevalent in our world.

And this is the condemnation, that light is come into the world, and men loved darkness rather than light, because their deeds were evil. For everyone who does evil hates the light, neither comes to the light, unless his deeds should be reproved. But he that does truth comes to the light, that his deeds may be made manifest, that they are wrought in God. John 3:19-21

Everyone can attain the experience of the Light of Christ, regardless of religion or cultural background. As human beings, this gift is part of our divine inheritance. The light knows only one barrier: the limited thinking and hardened hearts of human beings. When we truly let go and let God move through us, the increase of light is a natural consequence. When a large cauldron of metal is heated, the impurities in the metal rise to the surface, where it is cooler. These impurities, the dross, look like a scum covering the molten metal. This dross weakens the structure of the metal when it remains, so it must be purged out or skimmed off. The same is true with us. When the light begins to increase in our body, the impurities rise to the surface and must be released. If we are plagued by bad habits, negative thoughts, and fears, then they must be removed before the light can express through us purely. As in the case of the metal, we will also be stronger when this happens.

A while ago, I was heading a home remodeling project, and one of my employees expressed his disdain for sweeping the floor, complaining that it was a mindless task. I turned to him and asked, "If your mind wasn't there when you swept the floor, where was it?" It is possible to spend hours in prayer or meditation and be so involved in the spinning of the mind that no part of God ever gets through. Likewise, it is possible to perform the most menial, mundane tasks and to be so immersed in God that even sweeping the floor becomes a holy action. Our separating one job as meaningful from another as menial limits God's ability to work through us. Our ability to be mindful of God, even in the small tasks of life, allows divine purpose to flow through what we are doing.

We cannot truly love God if we feel that part of his creation is meaningless and worth ignoring. This is the very concept which got us into trouble in the beginning, with Adam and Eve. We humans decided one type of experience was better than another, instead of humbly accepting what our Creator was presenting to us. When our minds are someplace else, we are not concentrating, and no life can move through us. We go through the motions, but our heart and mind are not present.

Concentration is absolutely critical to any spiritual practice. No communion with God is possible without the ability to keep our minds on the subject we are attempting to experience. Keeping our attention on the light requires a great deal of control of our thinking, which means we will have to develop our character and do some things toward which we would not naturally be inclined. In other words, when we are asked to discipline ourselves, the discipline is intended to stretch us and make us grow. Not applying effort will make us lazy and keep us from claiming our divine inheritance. Although all spiritual growth and initiation occurs through the unmerited grace of God, our efforts create a place in us where God's grace can manifest.

One who makes a pattern must be extremely careful in every method and precise in each instruction. The pattern must be perfect, so that it can be used over and over again with assured results. The life of Christ represents the perfect pattern for all to follow who seek to return to our Father. Each step Jesus took, and every experience he went through, is an experience we too will have on our spiritual journey. Our personal experience may not be on so grand a scale as Jesus' was, but the essence will be the same.

For example, our conscious commitment to be one with God is demonstrated by the baptism of Jesus and God's acknowledgment of him as God's Son. Jesus' temptations following the baptism are the blueprint for the trials and tests we experience following our commitment to the spiritual path. Our relatives and friends may conspire to turn us from the direction we are beginning to follow. The world usually has trouble with our decision to put God first, and we must overcome its influence and objections.

And after six days, Jesus took Peter, James and John, and brought them up into a high mountain apart, and he was transfigured before them; and his face did shine as the sun, and his raiment was white as the light.
Matthew 17:1-2

Every step Jesus took upon the earth represents a step along the spiritual path which each soul must travel. Everything he experienced set the pattern for the experiences we will have as we move closer to God. The transfiguration of Jesus on the mountain, before the three apostles, was his Illumination, when the full Light of God filled and transformed his body. Jesus was the great wayshower, and those who follow him will find God, just as he told us. The betrayal, trial, scourging, crucifixion, death, resurrection, and ascension are the archetypal patterns for each human soul journeying home to the Creator.

On the individual level, the betrayal can take the form of rejection by a trusted friend or deception by an associate. The trial and scourging can occur through the very difficult situations with which we find ourselves struggling, struggles that serve to break our outer husk to expose the new germ. Sometimes our personal crucifixion and death is accomplished through close relationship with others in which we are forced to give over old, hardened ways of doing things. Or the crucifixion of the ego can occur more interiorly by some crushing blow to our sense of security or the loss of personal capabilities. In either case, the crucifixion is designed to destroy those parts of us which separate us from God and other people.

In order to come into union with our Creator, we must be stripped of our pride and selfishness. The outer husk must be broken off the new grain and separated, through shaking and agitating the seed. The whole grain must be ground into powder, like the action of scourging and the trial. Only the newly ground flour can adequately mix with the spiritual waters to become pliable dough in the hands of God. We are kneaded until we are flexible. Leaven or yeast is added in the form of light, which causes us to expand to become who we really are. Finally, we are placed in the heat of divine love, to be transformed into the living bread which will nourish and sustain the spiritual life of others who seek to be fed.

Some souls have such a thick outer husk that it is very difficult to see the divinity within them. Years upon years of limited thinking and fear have caused a thick shell to form, obscuring the light. There is a type of pine cone whose seeds require the intense heat of a fire in order to break through the tough outer shell and allow the seed to sprout. Some human souls require the same intensity of experience in order for the outer habits and thinking to be changed. Not all will require the same treatment during their training on the spiritual path.

Look to the way in which Jesus, the great teacher, attended to his disciples. He treated Judas differently than Phillip and Matthew differently than Peter. Each soul requires a different approach because of its uniqueness. This is why there are so many different schools and approaches to God. Each works in a different way and is effective for the people drawn to that particular way. And yet, there is unity even in this diversity. For when you remove the outer appearances and distill the essential ingredients, the archetypal pattern is the same for all.

Enter in at the straight gate; for wide is the gate and broad is the way that leads to destruction, and many there be which go in there; Because straight is the gate, and narrow is the way, which leads to life, and few there be that find it.
Matthew 7:13-14

The way to God is the same for everyone. Different paths may appear different, but this is just appearance. The process is difficult, because it requires letting go of concepts about who we are, without knowing what we are to become. The outer individual must die in order for the inner soul to be reborn in God. When the light begins to shine in our temple, a great fount of energy is at our

116

disposal. A regeneration of our body takes place, and we feel vitality and life flowing through every cell. We become, once more, a child of God in every sense. This life is God's life. The light must increase if we are to transform all of our old patterns. As we use the light to see, the veil of confusion lifts from our senses, and we begin to experience the mind of God more deeply.

As we seek to know the mind of God more, when we think of a subject, we can ask for the light to show up the important aspects about which we need to be aware. When we are praying, we can visualize this light shining around and through the ones for whom we pray. When we give someone a healing or a blessing, we can direct the light into that person, to fill him or her with the presence of God. This is what is meant by "working with the light." As with any skill, practice increases our abilities and makes us more confident of our connection with God.

God's nature is light, and in God there is no darkness at all. As we harmonize ourselves with God's presence and long for God to be more and more inside of us, the light increases proportionately to our desire and strivings. The closer we are to God, the more light we will see and feel within the temple of our bodies. This is natural and part of God's divine plan for us. To be without light is a disorder created by people who have knowingly or unknowingly cut themselves off from God.

To find the light within, spend time each day looking within. Look in the center of the body for the radiance of our eternal God. Keep your thoughts and desires quiet. As we direct our thoughts inward, instead of allowing them to be continually directed outward, we build up a certain energy stock, which in turn ignites the action of the light within our souls. The light has always been there, but it needs our attention and dedication in order to intensify and fill our bodies.

A young novice went to visit a holy man. The novice said, "Father, according as I am able, I keep my practice, and my little fast, my prayer, meditation and my contemplative silence. As much as I am able, I strive to cleanse my heart of impure thoughts. What more must I do?" The elder rose up and stretched out his hands to heaven, and his fingers became like ten lamps of flame. "Why not," he said, "be totally changed into fire?"

May the light of Christ come into you and dwell with you always.

ॐ

CHAPTER SEVEN
FAITH

Verily I say to you, if you have faith, and doubt not, you shall not only do this to the fig tree, but also if you shall say to this mountain, be thou removed, and be cast into the sea, it shall be done. And all things, whatever you shall ask in prayer, believing, you shall receive.

Matthew 21:21

Once I met a woman who had contracted multiple sclerosis when she was thirteen years old. At the time I met her, she was in her early thirty's and could only get around with a walker. She was a very strong woman, tough and articulate. When we talked about her illness, she described to me the traumatic experience which preceded the onset of the disease. When she was 12 years old, her father had bought her a bicycle. He drove her out about five miles from home, took the bike out of the car, and told her to ride it home. Then he drove off, leaving her stranded. The girl had little experience of riding a bike, but not knowing what else to do, she made a valiant attempt. She rode for three of the five miles, falling and picking herself back up time after time.

About two miles from home, she was so tired and sore that she sat down on the side of the road to rest. Her knees were raw from all the falls she had taken, and she felt wounded by her father's cruelty. Her father, feeling that she had taken too long, drove back in the car and stopped when he saw her. He reprimanded her for taking so long, and then he told her that if she did not get up and ride home before dark, he was going to return the bike to the store. She was scared, furious, and hurt. In pain, she got back on the bike and struggled the rest of the way home. After she arrived at home, she began to get sick, and, over the next few weeks, she came down with this degenerative disease of the spine.

As she related the experience to me, I could see that she was still enraged at her father twenty years later. Her anger had literally locked up her spine and prevented her from walking. It was as if she was giving her father the continuing message that what he had done was so horrible that she would remain physically damaged forever. The woman had some consciousness of this and admitted that she was getting back at her father through her illness. She had faith that her multiple sclerosis was paying him back for his cruelty, and she was going to get as much mileage out of this disease as possible. She expressed a great belief in the possibility of her own healing, but her stubbornness and lack of forgiveness toward her father prevented it.

Faith is knowing that the Laws of God work. The common conception about faith is that it is magically bestowed on certain fortunate people at birth, while others, perhaps ourselves included, are short-changed. The ones who receive faith are the religious types, and the ones who do not profess to be faithful are those who get along very well without religion. This superficial look at faith denotes a basic misunderstanding. Faith is not a vague feeling or a mystical, ethereal quality. In most religions, faith is seen merely as an adherence to a set of doctrines or creeds. This is not the type of faith I want to address. The faith which consists of a series of accepted ideas is not the faith that moves mountains. It is not the substantial faith of which St. Paul spoke.

For many years, we had faith in science, and the ability of scientists to prolong our lives and make them more comfortable. We had faith in nuclear energy and in the latest chemicals and medicines. Now, we are horrified at the potential danger of many of these inventions, and we fear for the safety of our loved ones facing the by-products

120

of these technologies. Our faith in science is still strong, but that is not substantial faith. Such a faith is transitory and fleeting, and, although it might make life easier, it does not bring a lasting peace.

Even so, faith, if it has not works, is dead, being alone.
James 2:14-17

Faith as an idea cannot sanctify you. Faith alone is unproductive if it remains merely an intellectual conviction. Faith longs for action. Faith is something we do which produces a result; it is not a set of beliefs which we learn in church. We exercise our faith every moment. When we get up in the morning and get out of bed, we have faith that the floor will support our weight. We have faith that the world we experience today will work the same way it did yesterday. When we were children, we saw older kids riding bicycles, and we told ourselves that, if they could do it, so could we. Then we tried it ourselves, and it worked. Even in the smallest things, we demonstrate faith.

Everyone has faith in different things, to different degrees. Some have faith in themselves and are not able to trust anyone else. They have learned that they are the only ones who really know what they need and what is best for them. Some have faith in material wealth, believing money will secure their life from tribulations. Some have faith in food or clothing, doctors or friends. Whatever we have faith in will be a source of fulfillment and security. Few have real faith in God, truly trusting God with their lives, no matter what they profess to the contrary.

And he was in the stern of the ship, asleep on a pillow, and they awoke him and said to him, "Master, don't you care that we perish?" And he arose, and rebuked the wind, and said to the sea, "Peace, be still." And the wind ceased, and there was a great calm. And he said to them, "Why are you so fearful?

How is it that you have no faith?"
Mark 4:37-40

Much like the apostles in Mark's passage, we relegate our faith to spiritual matters and attempt to take care of material things ourselves. Only when life throws us a curve and things are falling apart do we turn with imploring hearts to God. We are inconvenienced in our routine by having to acknowledge our inability to overcome a problem or to heal a disease on our own. When we are helpless to change something by our own power, we are humbled into asking God for help.

There is a lady I know who is bedridden and weighs 70 pounds. She has some disease that has confounded the doctors, and she prays all day long. Her husband prays everyday at church and makes sacrifices in order to obtain God's grace for her healing. This lady does not want to see anybody, because she is ashamed of her affliction. But she also is not willing to have her condition changed. She is suffering for a reason, paying something off in her own mind. She has more faith in her illness and its benefits than in the power of God to change her life and heal her body.

Religious people have a tendency to engage in what I call a "crucifixion complex." A crucifixion complex entails suffering for its own sake, enduring your suffering with a martyred smile, while having the conviction that you are becoming more holy in the process. In most cases, this affliction was not sent by God, but instead it is self-imposed. Usually this suffering makes life somehow more meaningful and helps the person feel that he or she can do something worthwhile for God. Asking God at the outset if this was an appropriate expression of devotion never crossed their minds. They have faith in themselves and in their condition, not in God. It would be a far different matter for God to send suffering that was holy and for a purpose than for you to create suffering because of your own limited and negative thinking.

People have faith in very different things. Whatever you have faith in will be your source of support and help. Eventually, if God is continually ignored, the things you have faith in will fall apart, be short-lived, or be somehow changed. For now, your faith gives you a reason to live. That reason may not always exist – for if that reason is not God, it is not eternal. If your faith is rooted in God, it will be lasting, permanent, and reliable.

Faith is the substance of things hoped for, the evidence of things not seen.
Hebrews 11:1

Faith is an act of the whole person. It begins with an assumption and grows into a result. Faith is the assumption that precedes knowing, which in turn precedes the realization of something. We have to start somewhere, so we believe that God is able to fulfill our requests. We believe that life is good and that God loves us and is watching over us. We believe that God is present in everything. But that is only the beginning. We really do not know these things yet. We hope for them and we rely on them, but we have not yet experienced them. Only experience brings knowing. This is why faith requires action – stepping out into the world in the trust that our needs will be met. Once we continually find that God is truly taking care of us, we have the experience we need to build the reality of our faith.

Once, I asked a group of people to share the one thing they knew beyond a shadow of doubt. What they shared could not be their opinions, hopes, wishes, dreams, or fantasies, but instead it had to be something of which they had knowledge through experience. All of them thought for a long time, and then they related one or two important bits of experience of which they were certain. One said he knew his prayers were answered, at least a couple of them. One woman said she knew she felt the divine presence when she meditated. Another said she knew she was loved by God. One woman simply broke down and cried. She said there was nothing of which she was absolutely certain. This was a very beautiful experience for this young woman. She realized at that moment that all the activities of her life had not brought her any closer to finding the truth. If life went on like this for her, it would end up being meaningless. Realizing that was a very humbling experience for her.

Ask yourself what you really know – from experience, beyond the shadow of any doubt. What you choose would have to be something that you would put your life on if you were called to, something you would die for or stand on no matter what, and no argument or convincing on anyone's part could change your position. The difference between opinions, guesses, and knowing is that knowing comes from something that happens to you which then becomes firmly rooted in your being. Opinions and guesses do not necessarily involve you, nor do they require you to change as a person.

Beliefs are the seeds of knowing. Beliefs are important – but by themselves, they do not satisfy. They provide the means for the first step towards faith, but they are not the end result. Beliefs are the scaffolding which is erected in order to build the whole house. The house erected is the knowing that comes from real experience. Through faith, we can arrive at certainty, but it takes experience to do so. Experience is the only thing that brings knowing. Experience of God brings certainty of God. Beliefs are merely the skeletal form, unclothed as yet in flesh. Faith yearns for what it does not see, and by its nature, it carries in itself some of the substance of the thing for which you strive. That substance is enough to draw you through your assumption to the experience of whatever you are seeking.

Here is how building with faith is much like building a house. When I want to build an addition to a home, I make a plan by setting my idea on paper. Then I have the foundation laid, which represents my decision regarding that for which I am praying. The frame has to be built next, so that the dwelling can be supported. Faith provides the support for the answer to prayer. It is the substance and evidence of what we do not yet see. If the house is not visible yet, the inner pattern of the house is. The activity of the fleshing in, or manifestation, of the walls and roof of the house is the working of faith, acting on the initial idea of wanting a home. We put our faith into manifestation when we create the form in which our prayer can manifest.

Faith must develop, before it produces that within which you have faith. If you have faith in wealth, then your faith increases by stages, bringing you ever closer to the experience of wealth. Your faith makes it possible for you to get the kind of employment that brings in large amounts of money. Faith puts you in contact with the right people. Faith and desire get you the appropriate training to do your job well. Your faith makes you begin to think of what you will do with your wealth. All of these develop out of that original assumption of wealth. This example applies equally well to anything in which you invest your faith.

If you have faith that God can answer your prayers, you will pray to God when you need something. Your assumption that God can do it is enough to get started. After you ask God, your faith is demonstrated in your acceptance and knowing of the fact that God is getting you what you want. Faith turns into certainty when you receive what you requested. Once you have experienced having your prayer answered, you know that God exists, that God responds to your requests, and that God can do the same again.

But Jesus turned around when he saw her, and he said, "Daughter, be of good comfort; your faith has made you whole."
Matthew 9:22

Faith creates a point of entry for the power of God to move through. A speck of faith that God can reach down and touch your heart is enough to allow an opening for this to actually happen. When you talk to God, have a little hope that you will feel God's presence when God listens to you. This mustard seed of hope will be enough faith for that to occur. One of my spiritual directors was fond of telling students that, every time they opened a door, they should expect to see Jesus. This exercise engenders hopefulness and puts our faith into practice. When I tried this exercise, I was very excited, and a little frightened. If Jesus actually would be there, what would I do or say to him? What would he see when he looked at me? As I did this exercise, I was fully expectant to see him, and years later I actually did. You can too, if you only have faith.

Faith comes by hearing, and hearing by the Word of God.
Romans 10:17

We hear about people who have visions of angelic beings or who have seen spiritual messengers. We read stories about people who have had the experience of clinical death. They have passed through death and seen that life is continuous. Some report having been to another realm of consciousness. Profound changes are reported in the lives of these people as a result of these experiences. Their conviction about their experiences becomes unshakeable, and important pieces in the puzzle of their lives are answered. Life is never the same again for those who have had a real experience. Those ones have graduated from belief, to knowing. Their experience demonstrates what is possible for all of us.

And Peter answered him and said, "Lord, if it be you, bid me come to thee on the water." And he said, "Come." And when Peter came down out of the ship, he walked on the water, to go to Jesus. But when he saw the wind boisterous, he was afraid, and beginning to sink, he cried, saying, "Lord, save me." And immediately Jesus stretched forth his hand and caught him, and said to him, "0 you of little faith, wherefore did you doubt?"
Matthew 14:28-31

That was possible for Jesus was possible for his apostles. If the apostles exercised the strong action of faith, their deeds would be like their Master's. Countless men and women throughout the ages have had similar experiences, healings, and other miracles through the strength of their faith. Mother Theresa was once asked how she could confront the multitudes of dying and starving in India without discouragement. "It is not my job to be successful," she answered, "It is my job to be faithful." Her faith in God's ability to reach the poor, to feed and heal them was so strong that thousands of people were moved to help her in this ministry. For them, the manifestation of shelter, food, clothing, and medicine was proof of God's recognition of her faith. This faith is the substance of what they hope for, the evidence of what is not seen.

Several years ago, I was visiting some friends one evening, when they mentioned that their young daughter was coming down with the flu, something everyone in the family had endured recently. The girl's head was aching, she was nauseated, and she was having trouble breathing. I offered to give her a blessing to relieve the distress. Surprisingly, her parents agreed. The father and the daughter brought me into a room away from the others, and I put both hands on top of her little head. I could feel the heat of her fever, as I prayed for this condition to lift and that she be completely healed. Then, I thanked God and Jesus for their assistance, and a little while later I left. After leaving, I forgot all about it; but the next day, I happened to be at the same family's house again, and they informed me that the condition was lifted. The girl had not come down with anything after all. The faith of the parents and the faith of the little girl drew the healing power of God into that situation to clear it up. I do not heal; God heals. God will heal through anybody whose faith allows him or her to become a vehicle for God's power and healing energy to move through.

If we love God, we will have faith in God's power and in God's ability to penetrate every aspect of our lives. If we do not trust God, we are likely to have a greater faith in our own abilities than in God, remembering God only when we are in trouble and have exhausted our personal resources. Do you have faith in yourself, or faith in God?

Through faith we understand that the worlds were framed by the Word of God, so that things which are seen were not made of things which do appear.
Hebrews 11:3

Here is an exercise you might want to try, in order to develop your awareness of how God works through you. This exercise will help you realize how important your thinking is, and it will develop your trust in God.

1. Pick some attribute or quality you want to develop in yourself. It can be as simple as having more energy as you go about your day, or as in-depth as wanting to be less selfish in relationships with other people. But I suggest you take something simple, like remembering your dreams or an appointment.

2. Right before going to sleep at night, create a direct command or statement concerning what you have chosen – what you want to develop. Make it an affirmative statement such as, "Tomorrow, I will give of myself in relationships;

Tomorrow, I will wake up filled with energy and vitality; Tomorrow, I will be completely aware of my appointment with so and so." Be specific, and form the statement as a gentle command.

Let us say you want to be kind to someone you know you have not been so kind to in the past. Your statement would be something like, "Tomorrow, I will be kind and loving to _____."

3. Before going to sleep, say this statement seven times, out loud, with conviction and feeling.

4. Go to sleep, allowing your affirmation to take root overnight. In the morning, it will be a paramount law for your whole being, and as such, it will manifest to you as an inner reminder.

The principle is simple and easy to apply. Your conscious mind is the decisive part of your thinking. When you make the statement, it goes into the subconscious as a command or a law, which will be worked on by the subconscious all night long. In the morning, the subconscious will have already complied by reminding you of what you decided to do the night before. The subconscious will have set up all the channels for this to be accomplished. One night, I asked a group of students to do this with the command that they remember their dreams during the night and that they be conscious of them when they awoke in the morning. During our following meeting, every one of the students who took the exercise seriously reported success.

Remember: repeat the statement with feeling seven times. Then, when you go to sleep, your mind will not have time to fight or interfere with the command given to your subconscious. You will be too tired to doubt what you are stating. Then, it will manifest in your life the next day. Affirmations are very powerful, and they demonstrate our right to access the power and energy of God. Faith is the motive power that sets this mental law into action. Jesus said that if we have faith the size of a mustard seed we will move mountains. If your faith is not yet moving mountains, do not despair. The substance of faith increases as it is put into action, bringing the evidence of what is yet unseen.

CHAPTER EIGHT

LOVE

... one of them put a question, "Master, which is the greatest commandment in the law?" Jesus said to him, "You must love the Lord your God with all your heart, and with all your soul, and with all your mind. This is the greatest and the first commandment. And the second resembles it. You must love your neighbor as yourself."

Matthew 22:36-39

When I was eighteen years of age, I was living in the Pacific Northwest. I had become involved with a group of spiritualists, people who allow discarnate spirits into their bodies to speak through them. During the day, I worked in a warehouse, and four nights a week, I attended meetings to listen to the messages given through these spirits. For a number of months, I had been attending these meetings faithfully and had begun to practice allowing myself to open up to psychic influences. In fact, I was becoming quite adept at giving clairvoyant readings during the public meetings and was beginning to draw the attention of the older spiritualists as one who held considerable promise.

One evening, an unknown woman showed up at one of our private group meetings. She was an older woman, probably in her mid-fifties, and very strong, with a clear, open face. The leaders of the group seemed to know her, but no one else had ever seen her before. She arrived late and sat down without speaking a word. She said nothing at all during the meeting, but when the session was over she came directly over to my wife and me and said, "I want you to know, there is nothing but light." We had no idea what she was talking about. I looked at her and said, "The sun comes up and it's light and the sun goes down and it's dark. I don't get it." I had absolutely no conception of what she was trying to convey. I remember feeling for a moment as though I was suspended in space. Her words struck a resonant chord in me that was, at that point, too vague and distant to grasp. Then, the woman simply repeated the same words and left. Although the experience was rather strange, frankly, I dismissed it and forgot about her.

Two weeks later, the same woman showed up at another meeting. Again, she arrived late, and again, she sat in silence through the meeting. I did not think much of her being there, until afterwards, when she came up to us again and said, "In God there is no darkness at all; there is only light." Still, I was having a major problem understanding what she meant. I felt as if I must be the most dense person in the world. So I asked her to explain what she meant, and she more or less repeated her message, saying that in the Universe there was no darkness at all, only light. Then she left.

Within two weeks of this woman's last visit, I began to experience some subtle, but potent, changes in my approach to the group. Soon, I began to notice how each of the five leaders of the various spiritualist groups all suffered from some form of spinal or lower back difficulties, which caused them to use canes, walkers, or wheelchairs. Then it occurred to me that, when they allowed discarnate spirits into their bodies, they were relinquishing their own volition, which was manifesting in their inability to move their lower limbs. Sometimes after coming out of the trances, they would temporarily lose the use of their limbs. I began to seriously question both who these entities were and the actual value of the messages they were transmitting.

In my time with the spiritualists, I had a number of experiences of allowing a spirit to use my physical body. The feeling I encountered was rather coarse and sensual. Usually, I would see a dull red as the being would enter my hands and arms, or somewhere on my spine. One experience my wife had with trance mediumship left her completely drained of energy for an entire day. She described feeling as though all of the life had been drawn out of her during the encounter. Most frightening of all was an experience during one of the weekly group meetings, when a member of the circle went into a coma during trance and required emergency transport to a local hospital. All of these things begin to add up in the dawning of my awareness.

And slowly, we began to realize the dangers inherent in playing with psychic fire. This nameless woman, who did not want to be known to us personally, did a great service in our lives. She loved God. She loved us enough to come and nudge us out of a potentially dangerous situation. Each time she visited our group, she traveled a long distance, seeking no recognition, and wanting nothing for herself. She came and gave a message which was meant to protect us from harm, and in so doing, she was expressing a selfless love.

The word "love" is the most abused word in our society today. The connotations of the word "love" run the gamut, from icy cold intellectual speculation about Divine Love, to the oil slick of sexual promiscuity. We use the word "love" to describe any feeling, whether selfish or altruistic. Usually the use of "love" implies longing or attachment. The word has been beaten, tortured, and kicked around for years. The concepts and mistaken opinions about love would fill volumes. Love is not a subjectivity, or a personal fantasy. Love is substantial like faith, and like faith, it requires action. But before we look at what love is, let us dissolve the misconceptions and see what it is not.

Here are some common misconceptions about love and how love is expressed and shared:

1. Love is never having to apologize or admit mistakes.
2. Love is God caring about me and never having any say or opinion about my actions, words, or thoughts.
3. Love is riding off into the sunset in a convertible with the person of my dreams. There has to be plenty of mist and slow-motion special effects with this one.
4. Love is having someone worship the ground I tread.
5. Love is worshiping the ground someone treads because that individual is the most important thing in creation.
6. Love is goose bumps and wishy feelings in your belly.
7. Love is being swept up by the person of your dreams (add mist and soft glow) and being rescued from having to make any more decisions about your life.
8. Love is sex.
9. Love is hot flashes and rushes throughout your body.
10. Love is passionate, unabashed feelings which break loose from the body in the evening and go out to any available object or recipient of those feelings.
11. Love is being protected from having to do what you do not want to do.
12. Love is getting your own way, because of your superior power and special qualities that make you the obvious decision-maker in a relationship.

Of course, I am being facetious when I list these myths about love. Love, of course, is none of these things. This is probably going to disappoint some of you, but love has nothing to do with fantasies, dreams, and wishes. If love were something communicably transmitted, then we could contract this disease from others. If love were a possession, we could purchase it. Love is neither a glandular explosion nor a material possession. All these misguided ideas about love can best be relegated to the romance novels and B-grade movies.

You may feel that discussing love is entering sacred territory. Or you may feel that the whole area should be roped off and reserved for your private thoughts. But private thoughts are not love. The secret thoughts about what you want from others, and what you want to do for and with others, is completely foreign to the concept of love. When you begin to love, it is common to wish to twist and mold the other person to fit into your projection and image. Sometimes, you feel the other person should worship you and be completely infatuated with you. You want the other person to focus on one quality or aspect of you which you previously decided was noteworthy. You want her to focus on that part of you forever, so that life will be rosy, blissful, and wonderful without any agitation of the waters. You do not want to shake apart any of the concepts hidden within your privacy. You definitely do not want to have the light turned up so that all of your faults are noticeable.

When we love, we do not fear. Love and fear are exact opposites. Love gives, fear defends and holds back. Fear cuts off and is suspicious; love trusts and does not doubt. Our fears, expectations, and pre-conceived ideas can only get in love's way. We need to remove our concepts of what we want and begin to take a fresh view of love. Love is not an emotion. The pleasant feeling we experience when we are helpful to someone is not necessarily love – it is a bodily response to our act of love. Love is born of our willingness, not of our desires.

When we are children, we look to our parents to love us and give us the affection and support we seek. For babies, this is especially important; but when we grow up a little, that kind of nurture and protection is less necessary. Those who do not receive this kind of maternal and paternal love still need it, and so they often seek it in intimate relationships. As babies, we need protection from heavy winds and from the storms of life. Everyone knows this feeling, either from memory or because we feel it now. We expect our ideal friend or lover or parent or teacher or priest to accept everything about us. They should make sure we never have to struggle with anything, and they must always hold us in highest esteem. Their job is to keep us from serious self-examination and overlook the words and thoughts that betray our humanness and selfishness.

The unexamined life is not worth living.
- Socrates

As we seek others with whom to be in relationship, we project onto them the qualities we feel we lack. We believe the potential beloved has the missing pieces to our lives. He or she completes what we are incapable of fulfilling alone. An example of this projection is in cases where children were placed with adoptive parents. Generally, these children have a problem with love. In their hearts, they realize that they were abandoned. Whether they know there was a good reason or not does not seem to matter. They were left alone, and the mother whose heartbeat they were accustomed to hearing in the womb is no longer present. She was warm and loving to them for a short time, and then all was gray and desolate. The adoptive parents do not have this bond, and they must struggle heroically to develop it. From the child's point of view, the emotional response to this experience is that, if mom could not continue to love me by being with me, then there is something unlovable about me. I am not worthy of love.

My experience in counseling has been to see this same pattern of suspicion and testing with people who have had neglectful, rejecting, or abusive parents. These people desperately want to love and be loved, but they think there is too much wrong with them for it to actually happen. Often they believe that those who love them are deficient in some way, because if those people are able to love them, they obviously do not see how unlovable they really are.

These people expect the worst, and what they are saying is, "go ahead, kick me – the meaningful people in my life had good reason to." Loving and being loved can be an especially painful experience for these people, and so they will challenge even the most loving and forgiving nature. Overcoming the pain of their early lives is an extended struggle.

Love suffers long, is kind; love envies not; love is never boastful, is not puffed up, does not behave itself unseemly, seeks not her own, is not easily provoked, thinks no evil; Love rejoices not in iniquity but rejoices in the truth; bears all things, believes all hings, hopes all things, endures all things. Love never fails.
I Corinthians 13:4-8

When we say "I love you," we are saying that we feel the power and energy of God trying to pass from us to the person to whom we say this. This is the Life Principle passing from itself to itself. This is the way everything is built in creation – everything is interconnected.

...God is love, and he that dwells in love dwells in God, and God in him....There is no fear in love; but perfect love casts out fear; because fear has torment. He that fears is not made perfect in love. We loveGod because God first loved us. If a man says "I love God" and hates his brother, he is a liar; for he that loves not his brother whom he has seen, how can he love God whom he has not seen?
I John 4:16-20

Our yearning for love comes from God's first loving us. God loves God's creation. For God's love originated in God's act of creating. Love is the divine attribute which always supplies through the same Law as prayer; if we love, we must be loved. Love creates a vacuum which must be filled. Love is a channel you create that links you with anything you want to know, or with anything with which you want to be united. Love is a decision to get to know something deeply. The power and energy of God flow through this channel which love creates between yourself and the object of interest. Through the consistent action of God's Laws, energy will always flow through this channel.

Love is the decision to know someone on all levels so completely that there is no more mystery. When a relationship with another person is involved, we want to know the other so well that we spend time and effort inquiring about them. Through our attentive love, information passes between us, in the channel created by our love for one another. Love also works the other way – it allows another to know you and experience you fully. When you really love someone, you are committed to knowing that individual completely. This is where it gets a little frightening. This love creates such a powerful channel that any and all information about the loved one passes through to be known by the lover. Sometimes, we become frightened, because the other gets to know parts of us which we felt were better hidden away.

God's love is the first love; our love is the reflection. The Creator loved and created us; we recreate the Creator through our love of God and humanity. Love is the give and take within the being of God. The same process of giving and taking is expressed sexually on the individual level. You cannot know anything unless you love it. If you wanted to know about airplanes, you would purchase books and magazines on airplanes. You would be thrilled with the idea of flying and flying machines. Your interest in flying creates a channel through which information and inspiration passes to you about airplanes. Your love is the channel through which everything becomes known. If you want to know Jesus or God or your brother or sister, you must decide to love them, and soon you will begin to receive love from them. Then you would know them. Love is the tie that binds you to the object of your attention and to the goal of your desire. It is the stabilizing force for the connection.

Greater love has no one than this – that a man lay down his life for his friends.
John 15:17

Jesus' supreme sacrifice for us was the love of God made manifest in creation. By it, all life was given hope, and a new pattern was begun for the earth. His humiliating death and painful rejection was the very price paid which reversed humanity's condition of separation from God. Jesus Christ cleaned the slate of error for everyone and bridged the gap between God and Man. Jesus loved us in the same way God does.

As the Father has loved me, so have I loved you; abide in my love.
John 15:5

When our love is true and strong, we will be in harmony with what God loves. Whatever God blesses must receive our love, since it comes from God. Many people have various ideas about who they feel is the best representative of God. Deciding which prophet, teacher, saint, or savior is better than the rest is more conjecture than a matter of importance. What really matters is that God has chosen various beings to come to earth over the ages, beings whose job it was to represent God. In a long line of tradition, we see Abraham, Moses, Zoroaster, Buddha, Krishna, Jesus, Mohammed, and countless others. Some were given very local or cultural jobs to complete, while some were given global ones. Each brought a teaching which demonstrated a new dispensation and activity for people to adopt. All obediently fulfilled the mission God appointed them to fulfill, and all ultimately drew people closer to God.

God sent Jesus to earth to perform the greatest mission of all. No other prophet did what Jesus did – neither the abundant healings, nor raising the dead, nor, most importantly, laying down his life. Take some time to study the lives of God's messengers and prophets, and verify for yourself what I am saying. The impact of this one life was so far-reaching and powerful for the whole world that we still are benefiting from the great gift he gave us while he was here. Looking at the people of earth from God's point of view gives you the perspective of seeing the gifts each of these servants of God brought to us. Collectively, the accounts of these servants of God represent the manifestation of God's love for us. The greatest teaching of Jesus Christ concerned the commandment that we love God and love our fellow human beings.

Charity is similar to love, but it has come to mean something more obligatory, more peripheral to our personal life. Charity can be bestowed on others without our being personally involved with them, whereas love completely involves us with other people. The word "charity" is used sometimes in place of love. "Charity" comes from the Latin *caritas*, meaning dearness, or love. Originally, it meant the act of loving God with a devotion which transcends our liking for any created thing. It also meant loving our brothers for God's sake. St. Paul speaks of charity, not primarily as the giving of alms, but more in the sense of the love of God manifesting in the natural inclination to serve those who are in need.

And though I bestow all my goods to feed the poor, and though I give my body to be burned, and have not love, it profits me nothing.
I Corinthians 13:3

The kind of love about which St. Paul is writing is totally unselfish. It is the kind required by Jesus, that we love our neighbor as our self. People often feel that loving God is

140

easy, but loving human beings is very difficult, because they are so imperfect. This is a rationalization. When we love God, we begin to see God in everything. We see God in nature, in people, and our experience of God grows to the point of seeing God everywhere. To love God and not love what God created is a contradiction. For love to be love, it must be in deed and truth, not word and tongue.

There are numerous speeches on brotherhood and articles on caring for people, but speeches are not acts of kindness or lending someone a needed hand. Love is knowing someone's predicament and doing something about it. If we started to love God, we would begin to learn about God. God would not be the judgmental taskmaster that we fear God is. God is not lying in wait to catch us in our selfishness or hardheartedness. God loves us beyond comprehension, and we cannot diminish God's love for us. We can only cut ourselves off from receiving it. If God can love us before we are perfect, we can love our brothers and sisters, since we are all similarly imperfect. If we truly love God, we will love our neighbors the same as God loves us and we love God.

Ordinary love is selfish, darkly rooted in desires and satisfactions. Divine love is without condition, without boundary, without change. The flux of the human heart is gone forever at the transfixing touch of pure love.
- Sri Yukteswar, Teacher of ParamahansaYogananda

If we are only concerned with our immediate family, religion, social strata or race, then we do not yet know how to love. If we rope off a territory of acceptable human beings and decide these are worthy of our love, we have cut off the rest by our decision. This kind of love is not of God. It will not do you any good to do any more penances. It will not do you any good to build the great church, because God has the whole world as His sanctuary. It will not do you any good to add any more quiet time in prayer. But I will tell you something which you can do to really pay God back for

141

the love God gives you so freely. Find someone as unlovable as you are, and give that person the kind of love God has given you. This is why Jesus said, "Love your enemies." Loving them makes them friends. Pride is at the root of all separation between people, one thinking oneself better than the other. God's love showers on the happy and the sad alike, and all human beings are equal before God.

Tolerance is not love. Certainly, neighbors can be troublesome, and we can build higher fences or put more insulation in the walls. This method of dealing with the neighbors is designed to make them innocuous and less intrusive in our lives. This is tolerance. In tolerance, we arrange for people to stay at a safe enough distance so that we do not have to be directly hostile to them. There is no desire on our part to understand them or get to know them or be kind to them. We are satisfied that we are good to them, because we have never actually attacked them verbally. With relationships across driveways and apartments as tenuous as this, should it surprise us that boundaries between countries are so important? These arbitrary separations between people, between countries, between religions, between races are just another form of tolerance, fear, and selfishness. Love your enemies and you will be dissolving the artificial, manmade barriers that separate us from each other.

It is impossible to speak of love without talking about sacrifice. Sacrifice is loving to the point of giving something to someone else that we would rather keep. The word sacrifice means literally to give up a part to receive the whole. Fasting is a good example of sacrifice. When we fast, we abstain from doing something, giving up our part in order to receive something greater. Those who fast from speech find that, in giving up their right to speak, they become more sensitive to the speech of others. Those who fast from food find that it cleanses the body and makes it more sensitive to spiritual forces. Many people are conscious when they fast that the food from which they abstain is being given to those who do not have enough to eat. This fasting is their love, manifesting in a sacrifice which deprives them of something they need, for the benefit of others.

Sacrifice occurs wherever divine love is manifest. It is present whenever we extend ourselves to another person; it is present whenever we extend ourselves to God. Love takes responsibility for other human beings. It takes on their burdens and helps them when they are unable to help themselves. Love is God's energy. Love God as both the Creator and the creation, and you fulfill God's eternal Law.

꙳

CHAPTER NINE
HEALING

And he showed me a pure river of the water of life, clear as
crystal, proceeding out of the throne of God and of the Lamb.
In the midst of the street of it, and on either side of the river,
was the tree of life, which bore twelve fruits and yielded her
fruit every month; and the leaves of the tree were for the
healing of the nations.

Revelations 22:1-2

Health is a state of mind. If our thinking is positive and in accord with the mind of God, no sickness is possible. Let us not discuss organic or inherited diseases here. These illnesses are a different story and require an understanding of the needs of the individual soul in order to appreciate them. Instead, I want to focus on health and healing in relation to the psychological, mental, and emotional illnesses to which our minds and bodies are susceptible. The power of our mind is absolutely superior to our body processes. The body is a willing servant to the directives of our mental and emotional life.

An example of the power of mind over body can be found in research done concerning addictive disorders. These can include addictions to alcohol, caffeine, nicotine, and other drugs. A person who has difficulty handling life situations often turns to one of these drugs for support and/or relief. Drugs keep the person from having to deal directly with the emotional turmoil. After some time, taking the substances becomes habitual. For purposes of analogy, consider the area where we feel numb to emotional problems as a band of frequency on a scale, say between 20 and 30 points. If we fall into this frequency emotionally, we feel conflict and pain. In such times, we are faced with sorting through and dealing with our problems, or we can numb ourselves to the pain. This numbing requires that we use a substance which puts our emotional functioning either up over 30 points (some sort of stimulant) or under 20 points, with a depressant. In either case, we will not feel the pain and will not have to deal with it, as long as we are taking the substance.

This process is repeated over and over, until the body is unable to support the accumulation of drugs and begins to break down. Meanwhile, the subconscious mind has turned on the alarm in our bodily house, and it is desperately trying to get a message through to the conscious mind to change the habit and deal with the problem. Dreams may be the only way the warning can get through, because our conscious mind has shut out all other avenues of communication with the subconscious mind. Only the conscious mind can change a habit. The body does exactly what the conscious mind allows it to do. In the Bible, there is a statement: "As a man thinks in his heart, so is he." This means that our thinking determines the way we are, how we act, what we feel, and what our body does. Physicians have told us for many years that over 75% of physical symptoms are psychosomatic, or created in our own minds.

Through my work as a psychotherapist, I realized that over 90% of all physical illness is based on psychological, mental, and emotional factors. A case in point is a young couple I saw in counseling for alcohol abuse a number of years ago. The husband, who was drinking 12 to 14 beers each night, was the identified client. Despite his drinking, he held down a fairly decent job at the factory where he and his wife worked. After a couple months of treatment, he resolved to quit drinking entirely. This he accomplished, and soon after, he decided to withdraw from treatment and pronounce himself well.

Three months later, I received a call from a physician in the emergency room where I was on call. This same man had checked in suffering from a severe headache and a large red rash all over his stomach. The doctor was confounded and attributed it to possible psychological problems. When I arrived and entered the room, I noticed on the nightstand a quart container of Pepsi, from which my former client sipped continuously.

We discussed his symptoms, as he was very concerned; then I asked him about the Pepsi. He explained that he drank a lot of it – typically three of these quarts throughout the day. When I asked him about other caffeine consumption, he stated that he and his wife each consumed a whole pot of coffee every morning before work, and then they made a gallon of iced tea for each of them to drink during the morning. All of this drinking throughout the day amounted to a phenomenal quantity of caffeine, which explained the headaches and mysterious rash. This man had simply replaced one addiction with another, accomplishing the same result: not dealing with his emotional problems.

This situation reminds me of something a healer once told me. When I asked how he knew what to work on first with a person's illness, he said, "If they complain of pains in the feet, check the shoes first." Often, there are simple explanations for the illnesses we experience. In the case of the man with the headaches, he had made a conscious decision to hide from his problems through chemical abuse. His physical suffering was simply a result of his emotional fear of having to look at himself and his life and be shocked with how much homework he had yet to do. The natural forces of his body were beginning to rebel against his neglect of these problems and his not confronting his own feelings. We discussed the whole process of honestly getting in touch with that pain inside, and he started to make the commitment to tackle what was troubling him. His true and full healing could only come through his willingness to change conditions in his thinking which were producing this need to escape through chemicals.

The common cold is another example of the power the mind has over physical conditions. Many people experience two or three colds each year. Some attribute these colds to changes in the weather, or to germs. In these attributions, what we overlook is the fact that the lymphatic system, which produces all the mucous in our bodies, stores our emotional backlog. When we get a little confused about our lives and where we are going, our nose starts to drain. When we feel sorry for ourselves, we start to sneeze and purge. This is a natural cleansing of the body through the lymphatic system. Persistent colds are not simply cleansings; they represent more entrenched problems. They involve more deep-seated emotional and mental patterns.

Each illness has an emotional and mental basis which will cause it to persist until the emotional imbalance is corrected. With a great deal of research, we can devise a list of illnesses and their emotional and mental causes; however, each person is different in his or her combination of symptoms. Let us consider headaches. Our heads ache in many different ways: migraines, pulsing in various parts of the head, or even an all-over-the-head pain. The cause is similar in each case. Either we are resenting someone or something in our life, or we are resisting having to deal with some person, idea, or thing. To decipher exactly which of these causes is operative takes deep scrutiny, but, whatever the case may be, as soon as we let go of our resentment or resistance, the headache will disappear.

Almost all illness can be alleviated by simply adhering to the commands of Jesus: to bless those who curse us, to love our enemies, and to forgive those who offend us. These actions may sound simple, but in reality, they can be very difficult to accomplish. Through the counseling process, I have had many clients grow in small steps and then come to a brick wall. At some point, their growth stops, because they refuse to forgive a significant person who has mistreated them in some way. No further therapy or healing is possible against such a decision. When people choose to hold on to their anger and hurt, God cannot enter and fill them with God's love and peace. There would be no room for those things, for all the space the anger and hurt occupies. Usually the person who has offended them must pay before they feel vindicated and able to let it go. But I wonder who is truly paying. I have seen cancers and tumors develop from very intense cases of holding grudges.

The mind is very powerful. If we decide to live a life which is out of harmony with God's plan for us, our body has to fight nature and God's plan for us. This fight sets up a tension in our flesh and emotions which produces a state of stress or disease. If this tension persists, the disease will result in observable, physical symptoms. What was hidden in the mind and feelings soon rises to the surface and manifests in the physical body, appearing for all to see.

There is a story about Abraham Lincoln talking to one of his aides. Lincoln made mention of the deep lines on somebody's face, and the aide objected that no one was able to do anything about their facial lines. Lincoln replied emphatically, "By age 40, everyone is responsible for the lines on his face." Our thinking produces a definite effect on our body. We inherit a genetically endowed potential at birth, but what we do with that after 12 years of age is up to us. Before age 12, parents are programming us with their values and thinking, and the environment also has a major influence. At 12, we begin psychologically charting our own course and will have to live with the consequences of our own thinking.

There are no accidents in creation; everything has a cause, albeit a mysterious one at times. There is a reason for everything that happens to us, if we have eyes to see it. This is very frightening to some people, because it suggests that the predicaments we get ourselves into are our responsibility. If we are feeling bad, it is a feeling we have inadvertently created or allowed to occur. In order for someone to offend us, we must allow ourselves to be offended. Instead, we could just as well decide not to let it bother us. That we have these choices is, for many people, too much power and too much responsibility. We have complete power over our thoughts, emotions, and actions, and how we relate with the world and other people.

At this point, I can hear the question: "What would you do if someone were to pull out a gun to shoot you?" Well, I would certainly be concerned about the situation. I would quickly examine myself to determine if I had offended this person in the past and, if I had not, I would try to talk him out of shooting me. If I had offended him, I would apologize and ask forgiveness. If the person was adamant about persisting, I would have to place my trust in God and hope for the best. I might even try running away to avoid the experience, but I would not hate him or feel any need for revenge. All actions have an appropriate consequence. Whether that consequence takes place sooner or later, God has the entire situation well in hand. Knowing the day or hour of the fruition of the inexorable law of cause and effect is not up to us. "Vengeance is mine," says the Lord.

Human beings are such reactive creatures. We feel personally vindicated if we right a wrong or correct somebody. We feel their offense against us justifies cruel and unkind behavior, to get through to them and teach them a lesson. Retribution produces very serious illnesses if we persist in it. When we forgive somebody, even before they ask, we are allowing peace and blessings to flow to the offender and, invariably, we will feel this same peace.

Healing ourselves and others involves letting go and letting God work through our bodies, emotions, and thinking. We do not heal - God heals. The power, energy, and vitality of God are the only healing agents in creation. We can become

150

channels for that healing energy, letting it move through us freely. But the energy gets cut off from us when we try to take possession of it. Healing requires bringing the spiritual body back up to full charge, after it has been worn down by errors of thinking and feeling.

The spiritual body is an exact counterpart of the physical. When we are ill, it is because we are preventing the life force of the spiritual body from infusing and vitalizing our fleshly form. Most of the time, our conscious intention is to remain healthy, but subconsciously, we can use illness to escape confronting our problems. Sometimes we are not aware of thoughts which are producing an imbalance in our body. Whatever the case, being sick is the result of mis-thinking. As soon as we change our approach, clear up some confusion, or lift our feelings, the illness subsides and health is restored.

Continued errors of feeling and thinking produce a condition bordering on death. Many people suffer from the mistaken notion that they have no control over these conditions. After years of cutting off God's healing force and resisting the changes we need to make in our lives, our body creaks and strains to a slow halt. If the spiritual life force is prevented from moving into our bodies because of the way we think and feel, then our soul will eventually decide to vacate its home and find another home through which to express.

Jesus refers to those ones who are so cut off from the spiritual life force as the "walking dead." Their eyes are dark and lifeless, and no one is really home inside. They seem to be in a borderland of dreams and hallucinations, what psychology describes as the psychotic, schizophrenic, or borderline types. Their situation is quite serious, because they have abdicated responsibility for their own lives. They merely withdraw into themselves until withdrawing becomes a way of life. The dying process

151

begins. Admittedly, I am generalizing here about various mental illnesses; however, I am focusing on the more extreme disorders. Illness is a relative thing, the beginnings of which can be quite elusive and almost imperceptible. With the passage of time, the seriousness of a condition prevails and worsens, if the cause is not changed.

Healing can be channeled through a wide variety of agencies. In fact, anything that causes people to change for the better can be a healing agent. A book, a magazine, a friend, a movie, a symphony, a play, or a walk in the woods can be the healing channel. Whatever gets the condition healed is a healing instrument. These things can be random and unplanned at times. What we should strive for is some scientific approach which allows us to obtain results from our method of healing each and every time. Just as we want to be able to pray and receive an answer each time without fail, we want to be able to heal others and be healed each time.

The first method of healing is visualization and mental imagery. Some call this method absent treatment. We simply place the person and condition in our mind's eye and concentrate on them. We place our whole attention on them until we can see, feel, and sense them thoroughly. We visualize the condition changed into what we want, and we hold that new pattern in mind for that person or thing. We then see it being done and ask God to take care of its completion or fulfillment. For example, when you know someone who lives far away, you can use this method to obtain for that person a change of health or life conditions.

When my father-in-law was in the hospital for cancer of the bladder, we used this method. We spent a few minutes each day for about a week, praying for him and asking that his cancer be healed. We asked that the cause within him be removed and changed, and we visualized his bladder as whole and healthy. We asked God and Jesus Christ to accomplish this for him and us. He was scheduled for surgery, and during the operation, they found only a small, pea-sized tumor which could easily be removed. He had no subsequent difficulty with cancer. Through the healing prayers of a few people, he received a renewed hope in life, without which he might have resigned himself to dying.

Another method of healing is through laying our hands on a person's shoulders or head and allowing the power of God and God's Spirit to flow through us into the person. We are not the source of life and energy – God is. We simply clear our minds and focus on the needs of the person. We contact the Father and ask God for what we want for the person. Then we get out of the way and let the power, force, and healing life of God flow through our hands into the person to produce the healing.

This can be especially powerful with children, who are naturally open and receptive to the idea. They understand the power that can come through a touch. In fact, the fingertips of the hands are full of energy. The hands are natural conduits for healing energies and can be used as the way to direct God's power into a person in need of God's energy and healing.

...they shall lay hands on the sick, and the sick shall recover.
Mark 16:18

And one of them hit the servant of the high priest and cut off his right ear. And Jesus answered and said, "Put up your sword." And he touched his ear, and healed him.
Luke 22:50-51

...they brought forth the sick into the streets and laid them on beds and couches, that at least the shadow of Peter passing by might overshadow some of them. There came also a multitude from the cities round about to Jerusalem, bringing

sick folks and them which were vexed with unclean spirits;
and they were healed everyone.
Acts 5:15-15

A word of caution: be careful not to use your hands to sensitize yourself to the person in a receptive way. A lady I once knew was very receptive and sensitive like this, and she would always be picking up other peoples' conditions. If anyone felt nauseated around her, she would feel nauseated and ask who felt that way. When she was healing a person of a headache, she felt the pain move up her arms, and then she would feel her own head aching. In this, she was merely tuning herself into the person's ailment, and thus she was getting a good personal dose of it.

Healing, instead, involves letting God's love, peace, and life move into the person being healed and holding that pattern until the power ceases to move. At this point, the healing is complete. If we are coming down with the same condition that the person we are healing has, then we have done something wrong. We have gotten ourselves in the way, and the healing will not be successful. In every discussion of healing, the question arises: "What if it doesn't work? What if the person doesn't believe it can happen?" Indeed, if there is not sufficient faith in the possibility of being well by either the loved ones or the person who is ill, then the healing will not be able to occur.

God will not force us to change and does not want to take something from us we feel is valuable. If we value our sicknesses, God will respect that decision. If the healing does not work, there are three possible reasons. The failure may be because of the inability of the healing instrument to allow God's power to move through, or it may be because of the lack of openness of the person being healed. Sometimes the illness is needed by the person in order to grow. The reasons for failure of healing can only be one of these three things. If we are getting in the way of the healing by thinking that we are doing it ourselves, then the healing force will be cut off. If we are not open to God's power moving through us, it will not be able to move. Our cooperation with God is necessary for the healing process to be successful.

There are some organic and neurological diseases which the soul has accepted in order to grow and develop. We may look at people who have been in wheelchairs all their lives and feel sorry for them. These types of conditions are very trying for relatives and can sorely try the patience of the person afflicted. But let us look at the lessons that are being learned through this experience. When we are not able to locomote or stand up, we are confined to an entirely different outlook on the world. The experience develops patience and understanding, which the soul may require. When we are unable to communicate effectively with our voice, we are forced to learn to use feelings and touch to communicate. Loved ones must learn patience and courage in facing the difficult situation of caring for a handicapped person. They learn to trust more fully in God's plan.

These inherited disorders are purposeful from the standpoint of the soul. The soul needs a body that does not work correctly in order to develop within it certain qualities of character that it feels are missing. The soul is aware of the problems which are present in the developing fetus. The soul, drawing on the divine wisdom of God, may choose to inhabit a body which may be defective, in order to accomplish a particular purpose. We need to train ourselves to look past physical limitations to the deeper purpose being served. In this way, we need to cultivate what Jesus called "righteous judgment," rather than judging only by appearances.

There has been an increase of interest in health- related issues in the recent past. Many people spend much of their lives in trying to "stay healthy." Staying healthy is an important concern. However, we have made a god out of food and exercise in our culture. We spend plenty of time and money on exercise and diet programs to keep ourselves trim and healthy. What we have really accomplished is to exalt the physical body. We have made physical fitness our golden calf. We take vitamins and tranquilizers; we jog and work out compulsively; we watch our cholesterol and fat intake; we are wary of MSG and preservatives; and we talk a lot about stress. It is ironic that all this fear of unhealthiness contributes a great deal to our level of stress, which in turns robs us of our health. While it is important to be conscientious in what we eat and to keep the body toned with exercise, we need to understand that the most important factor as far as health is concerned is our thinking. Thinking affects the body no matter what vitamins you are taking.

And he called the multitude and said to them, "Not what goes into the mouth defiles a man; but what comes out of the mouth, this defiles a man."
Matthew 15:10-11

After giving the above teaching, Jesus goes on to explain that all the evil which we experience in our lives comes from our hearts and longings. Disease does not come from what we ingest, but instead it comes from errors in our thinking and feeling. When we clear up the struggles we have in our hearts, we pave the way for a healthy body. Granted, there are some things which we need to watch as far as what we take into our bodies. Water makes up 70% of the substance of our body and 90% of our brains. We are water-based creatures, and thus we require a steady flow of fluids into our body in order to live. Many of the illnesses we experience can be alleviated by large amounts of fluids which serve to cleanse and lubricate the body. There are times when removing meat from the diet is needed in order to help the body become more sensitive to spiritual influences. As well, when we are preparing for baptism or a

156

spiritual retreat of some kind, it may be wise to curtail the intake of meat or fatty foods, in order to make the body more receptive to the Spirit.

The healthiest combination of activity for your body is to drink far more water, eat a balanced diet with plenty of vegetables, and exercise through walking or other activities requiring some aerobic exertion. The other element required for a healthy body is proper breathing. Breath and spirit are synonymous terms in many languages. Through the breath, the Spirit passes into our bodies through the many light particles present in our atmosphere. Some people can actually see the Spirit in the air around them as small yods of light. These are light particles which pass into the lungs and into the blood to revitalize and regenerate bodies with the Spirit of God. When we breathe deeply from the belly and lower diaphragm, we are fully cleansing our lungs of used, stale oxygen and allowing a full change of fresh air into our lungs. We find when breathing deeply from the belly in this way that our minds are clearer, our bodies are more at peace, and our circulation is enhanced and vitalized.

Once, I was demonstrating full diaphragmatic breathing to someone and, as she began to breathe, she felt tingling in her head and down through her arms. She felt a little dizzy and much more relaxed, because she ceased to cut off the oxygen from her brain and extremities through her tense shoulder breathing. Once the full breathing begins, the whole body sighs and groans with relief. Deep breathing makes us feel better, because the peace we experience helps us slow down the rapid-fire frontal assault of thoughts we are accustomed to channeling through the brain. As we breathe more deeply, we feel more relaxed, and we do not have as much need for the flurry of ruminations and thoughts, so life becomes more simple and clear.

We receive the life force through the breath. The red blood cell has no nucleus that we can physically see, because the nucleus is a spiritual one. The red blood cell carries the vital life force through the body to all the cells and organs. This spiritual nucleus is charged with each breath, through the combination of lung and heart, on its journey around the vascular system. The red blood cell comes back to the heart spent and exhausted, and it leaves rejuvenated and filled with light and life. The reaction of breath with the life spark in the air ignites and charges the red blood cell and gives it renewed life. The red blood cells carry our personal experience, and they interact with the spiritual body to transmit this experience to our souls. This is the reason why spirit and breath have been used almost interchangeable in many cultures. *Ruach* is from Hebrew; *Pneuma* is Greek; *Prana* is the Sanskrit, each referring to spirit and breath.

If we would learn to breathe correctly and take in plenty of water, we would accomplish most of what is required to be healthy. Using basic common sense also facilitates maintenance of health. We must learn to be sensitive to the body's limits and protect it from environmental harm. The rest of the maintenance work is achieved by having a pure heart and being free of resentments, grudges, and fears. We must deny the thoughts that are negative and hurtful. We must evict them from the house of our thinking and bring in new, acceptable tenants, those which will make the new home feel whole and good. The stale things we store in the recesses of our hearts are the things which spoil our bodies and make our lives miserable. No person or thing outside of us can cause this to happen to us. Our health is our responsibility alone.

When we discover how bad we have made our lives, we need to call on God to help us remodel our dwelling place and change the very cells of our body. In my experience, people have only one major problem, if they have any at all.

Sometimes I tell people they do not have any problems, in order to give them a chance to stop attending to them and making them bigger. A teacher once told me that, if I wanted to have a problem, I should start thinking of one and it would grow. If we can take our minds off our problems and think loving thoughts, it will surprise us how good things can feel. Our attachment to ruminating about our difficulties is what feeds them and makes them escalate into life and death matters.

People do usually have one main hurdle to overcome, something which can be described as a character flaw. The other smaller problems are not the real problem – they are spokes of the main hub of the wheel. If spiritual pride is the real problem, the spokes might be fighting with various priests, ministers, parents, or other authority figures about some perceived wrong. We might distract ourselves by blaming others and focusing on what others are or are not doing to help us. The real problem is that we think we are special or more worthy of love than others, or any of a number of assumptions. Pride boasts of its own worthiness and greatness, secretly holding others to account for their imperfections. As demonstrated by Lucifer's fall from grace, pride is the father of all separation from God.

In healing an individual, it is necessary to develop spiritual sight, so that we can see the cause of the problem. Sometimes, we are prevented from seeing and still can ask for the condition to be lifted or the sin to be absolved. Try not to stumble over this last statement. Anyone who knows, loves, and serves God can ask, through the authority of Jesus Christ, that sins be lifted and forgiven. If we are sons and daughters of God, then we can heal and forgive, just as Jesus taught his disciples.

There is little difference between teaching, counseling, and healing. Each function helps people overcome their problems and teaches them to live in a fuller, more free

159

way. Healing is that which brings wholeness. Our instructions can teach a better way to live and thereby alleviate the need to experience negative conditions. Our counseling will help people resolve emotional conflicts and sort out negative feelings, with forgiveness and letting go as retroactive occurrences. Our healing work will allow the mind and body to function in harmony with God and to let go of the toxins we have built up through our mis-thinking.

Psychological research into the effects of color on mood and attitude has revealed that we are deeply affected by color in our environment. In one study, when prison cells were painted a light hue of pink, violent prisoners became compliant and gentle. Red rooms escalated the prisoners' violent behavior. The same findings have been found with severely mentally disordered patients, where blue is found to sooth and quiet them, while red adds to their agitation. Soothing combinations of soft light-green, blue, peach, and "sunny" yellow are replacing the monotony of sickening greens, pale grays, and dark beige in institutions. Light blue in a bedroom brings a more restful sleep, while peach and light orange pastels bring increased ability for mental and scholastic work. Cheerful colors enable us to feel positive about life, while somber, dull colors make us tend to depression. Pure white is often too stark and may cause discomfort if we have to live with too much of it. If white is softened with amber tones, its effect is more comfortable.

The color of the clothes we wear reveals our attraction to various colors. We need to choose colors which raise our spirits and make us feel good. Usually, we know what our favorite colors are. These are the ones we need to surround ourselves with and the colors we should wear. For a long time, I felt that I would get irritable when driving our new red car. Then I realized that the color was rubbing me inharmoniously and was changing my mood. When I realized this, we sold the car and bought a blue one. Then I felt much better. Yet, others might benefit from the clearer reds, as red tends to increase the vitality and energize the whole system.

Music produces a vibratory rhythm in our body which causes our cells to resonate with the sound and beat. If the beat is intense and chaotic, we experience that chaos within us. If the music is uplifting and harmonious, we enjoy its healing and balancing effect. There has been a lot of research on the effects of music on growing plants. Individual species of plants seem to thrive with different kinds of music. The same is true for people. Some people who are grouchy and angry would be aided by music that soothed and brought peace. Others might benefit by stimulating, motivating music, like marches and intense beats. Each person can benefit from different qualities of music at different times, depending on how that individual feels and what is needed. Researchers are just beginning to look at applications of music in the workplace.

Music is God's language, and it can thus heal the soul and body if applied carefully. Color represents the spectral variations of the one light of God manifested in creation. Through music and color, we can modify and change the very cell tension of our bodies, thereby altering our health. When we experiment with different colors and music, we can more accurately discern the colors and music which best suit our needs. As we grow closer to God, our sensitivity increases, and we begin to be drawn to more refined music and lighter, clearer shades of color in our surroundings.

Future discoveries will connect musical tones, color, and personality type to determine appropriate healing combinations for each individual. Each musical note has a color counterpart which, when combined (the music with the color) will further aid the medical profession in healing human beings when they experience illness. Some primitive investigations of filtering the light of the sun through various colored filters have produced some startling results. Blue light seems to bring peace and calm, while green light brings a balance and harmony to the body. These light treatments, combined with music compatible with the individual, might bring very successful results for healing.

The universe has provided us with all the necessary agents to bring about healing of our bodies and minds. We have herbs which form the medicines to combat illness, the sunlight and fresh air to energize our spirits, water to wash away toxins and keep our cells healthy, and human examples of selfless service who demonstrate harmonious thinking and feeling. Everything that would show us how to be and how to live is available, if we would but look and learn from life. Music, color, and light become tools at our disposal that will aid us in harmonizing our lives to God. Only in accord with God's pattern can we hope to have a healthy mind and body. In the final analysis, our health reflects our thinking, feeling, and attitudes, which puts the responsibility for being healthy on us.

꣣

CHAPTER TEN
OVERCOMING LIMITATION

*But the hour comes, and now is then, when the true
worshipers shall worship the Father in spirit and in truth; for
the Father seeks such to worship God. God is a Spirit; and
they thatworship God must worship God in spirit and in truth.*

John 4:23-24

Nothing outside of us can make us happy. We must look to God residing deep within us for peace and resolution of problems. In order to master the circumstances we confront, an inner battle must be waged, and we must vanquish the beast. The beast is the shadow side of our personality – all that seems frightening, dark, and negative. The roller coaster ride of emotional extremes keeps us from experiencing the poise and balance that can only be attained by becoming who we really are – the soul/Self. Firm, gentle love is the only means to train and direct the desires of the body. The body is not evil; but without a responsible tenant, it creates havoc by wanting things which are not essential. The nature of the flesh is such that it attempts to satisfy whatever it wants. Untamed and unbridled, it becomes addicted to habits. The body can be a willing servant of the mind; but after years of your allowing the body to have its own way, it rebels against training and changing.

Our seeking after emotional stimulation has reached such heights that many of us only feel alive if we are viewing a horror film or hearing an intense music concert. We seek more and more of whatever stimulates us. As we are stimulated, we give our personal power and responsibility away, to a play which evokes our tears, or to a comedy that provokes our laughter, because we are incapable of entering that depth of feeling by ourselves. We allow stimuli from outside of us to evoke feelings to which we have become numb within ourselves.

We might learn about ourselves through such experiences; we may even gain insight into our purpose here on earth. But this is usually not the motivation behind such activities. Instead, we desire this intensity of feeling in order to feel truly alive. We could learn a great deal from studying the ups and downs of our emotional life. The first observation we might make is that, when we are especially exhilarated and excited, we are heading for a compensating deflated and down-in-the-dumps experience. When we learn to even out the oscillating curve of our emotional highs and lows, we discover more peaceful harmony in our daily lives. When the body demands and complains, take it in hand like an unruly child, and firmly tell it to wait. The ability to delay gratification is an indication of our ability to exercise emotional control.

On the other hand, using harsh forms of abstinence will only produce a reaction on the other side of the scale. Harsh treatment of the body implies inherent fear that our bodies will cause harm to ourselves or others. It encourages the cycle of ups and downs and throws the body out of balance. Indulging the body eventually spoils it, while depriving it will unnecessarily weaken it. Moderation in the care of the body is far more effective. The body must be trained and mastered, to make it a willing servant and strong vehicle for the soul.

If your thoughts act like rebellious, uncontrolled children, ask God to help you quiet them, and channel those energies constructively. Jesus taught that we should not resist evil. Fighting the things which we dislike does not help matters. Resistance only makes the hated thing larger and more unyielding. When we fight the negative patterns, we bind ourselves inextricably to our own faults. When Jesus says we should not resist evil, he means we should turn away from it, not fight it. If we turn toward our own goodness and create new patterns within ourselves to replace the negative ones, then we overcome evil with good. There is no fight at this point, just a change of mind. We need to think of our negative traits as pockets of darkness into which the light has not poured. When we turn the light on a problem, the real truth inherent in the dilemma reveals itself. We can only hope to tackle one problem or dark spot at a time.

With men it is impossible, but not with God; for with God all things are possible.
Mark 10:27

If we do not take control of our desires and thinking, they will take control of us. When we do not like the things we see in our world, we have a choice: to let them happen, or to ask God to change them. If we enlist God's help, we must be willing to be the channels through which that prayer or wish is fulfilled. If we want someone to change, we have to be willing to speak with that person and inform him or her of the things that offend us. We put ourselves on the line for the changes we want in our lives. Our body and mental attitudes are the true cross which we must pick up daily in order to follow God. The outer ego and body consciousness must be crucified in order to release and liberate the inner, spiritual being.

When we step consciously onto the spiritual path, we are initiating the process of our own death. This death is the changing of the old habits, opinions, and thinking which caused our separation from God. Everything we have experienced up to that point was designed to frustrate us with life as it was, to increase our desire for oneness with God. All our trials were designed to bring us to our knees in recognition of our Creator. Only in God can our soul and body be at peace. Just as the north and south poles of the earth contain a positive and negative charge, so too do the body and spirit have opposite magnetic charges. The body is of the "dust of the earth" and carries a negative charge, while the Soul/Self is of the realm of heaven and carries a positive charge. By this analogy, we can see that the spiritual energies of the soul penetrate the flesh and regenerate it.

When our problems and concerns become so magnified that we are absorbed by the petty concerns of the world, the energies from the spirit are cut off. The body then feels like it is in charge and takes control of our lives through its indulgences. When the master within the soul is sleeping, problems and troubles increase. This is the reason we experience an ongoing argument inside of our heads about what we want versus what we are going to do. The war within results from giving far too much power to the body and desires to decide our fate.

Perfection in the physical world is unlikely. The earth is the school of experience for wayward souls who have forgotten their Creator and lost consciousness of the purpose of life. The earth has been humorously called the "reform school of the solar system," meaning that, here, the hard lessons of cause and consequence are lived out in the confines of the slow-grinding mill of time. No thought or action is exempt from its consequence, and every thought and action is our prayer. Yet, here on earth, causes and their effects are often much removed from each other, as the denseness of matter slows down the movement of spiritual law.

If we want to see into our future, we need just look at the fruits of today's thoughts and deeds. The future lies like a seed within those activities, knowable to those trained at looking beyond the surface of appearances. Despite the difficulties of doing so here on earth, strive we must, to attain that perfection which is our birthright. Unity with God is our goal and end. Each experience we have here in flesh determines the length of time our process of unfoldment will take. Some seem to travel the path back to God much faster than others, even though all souls start out at the same place. When inertia sets in and our life becomes inundated with habit, necessity and catastrophe seem to jerk us awake and motivate us to examine our lives. The limitation we feel during those times of crisis startles us and frightens us to do something constructive. Often, we must look to God and ask God to help extricate us from the backlog of our own predicament. If we stubbornly resist growing, nature will send many unforeseen experiences our way in order to wake us up.

As a child, I lived in a Midwestern city where there were frequent tornadoes. During one particularly intense storm, a tornado touched down in a residential section and destroyed three or four homes on one side of the street, jumped over to the other side to ruin another, then moved back to destroy still more. The houses that were saved along the street formed a jigsaw pattern which was truly phenomenal. I was awed by the intelligence of the storm in saving some houses and ruining others. Nature is inexorable in its ability to be tolerant of the human beings which live within it. It patiently teaches through its laws of cause and effect. For those without the desire to love or acknowledge God, nature will be their teacher. However, those few who desire a close, personal relationship with God will learn the lessons faster and more thoroughly. They will be able to overcome limitations much more quickly, because they have humbly recognized their need for help from their Father-Mother God.

In your patience do you possess your souls.
Luke 1:19

Circumstances and people annoy us only to the degree that we give them our attention. When we look away and stop giving other people power over our decisions, the irritation ceases. If we feel a particular emotion, we are responsible for that feeling. Others may try to offend us, but if we react, it demonstrates our own misunderstanding or lack of control. We must resist the temptation to blame and pass judgment, because the law of cause and effect is immutable in its action, and we will experience the same in kind.

Temptations come to all persons, no matter how holy their natures, and no matter how dark. A temptation is never more powerful than our ability to grow through it. God leads us through our temptations, which come from within our own hearts and desires. To desire something is not wrong, but to become attached and possessed by the object of our desire is to have a false god. In extreme cases, our attachment and possessive desires become obsessions. We need to desire what God wants for us, in order to steer clear of what is irrelevant for our spiritual growth. This is how we avoid temptation.

Jesus was tempted immediately after his baptism, when he went to fast and pray for forty days in the desert. His temptations are the same basic temptations we will all experience – those of the flesh, ambition, and pride. He was tempted to turn stones to bread, have glory and power over all the rulers of the earth, and to test God's ability to safeguard him from harm. We go through our own personal versions of these temptations. We want sensual gratifications as we indulge our bodily appetite and power among our fellow human beings. We are tempted to believe that all of our talents and gifts are self-developed and due to some intrinsic worthiness.

Perfect examples of those who struggle with these temptations are people who consciously begin the process of their own spiritual unfoldment. Maybe they have found a teacher or an order or a school to instruct them. They begin to look down on everyone else who is not consciously striving spiritually to know God. Their pride manifests in a sense of self-righteousness and in dangerous judgment of

168

other people. They believe their attainment is due to their own efforts, without acknowledging the movement of God's grace in drawing them closer. Instead, they should be thanking God for saving them from the errors which they could easily be experiencing if it were not for God's grace. Temptation is purposeful and vital to our development. It tests our faith and confirms our conviction in the direction we have established. Temptations provide the opportunity to strengthen within us those things we are striving to attain.

Forgiveness is probably the one thing which, if developed, would help us to overcome most of the difficulties we confront. When we mull over a problem, it gets bigger. If we would take the hurt and anger we feel, turn it around, and look at the situation from the other person's eyes, we would have a perfect opportunity to turn our curses into blessings. An effective assumption to make about people is that they sincerely mean well in all of their interactions. Most people are sincerely trying to do what is right, and any hurt which is inflicted is generally unintentional. Even if the other person appears to be inflicting intentional hurt, there are deeper, unconscious motivations that are eclipsing the higher nature. Just let go of the negative feelings for a second, and realize that the other person did not mean to hurt you and was not aware of how much you were hurt. Then bless them, and have God fill them with God's love and peace. In this way, we bless ourselves through transforming destructive feelings.

Often, we must speak with the other person and relate our feelings, and this takes some courage. Usually, the last person we talk to about our offenses is the one who caused them. We tell everyone else first and get as much support as we can for our one-sided assessment, and then we forget to talk to the real culprit. The person who offended us usually has an important bit of feedback for us which might make us grow in our dealings with others in the future. In

Matthew 18, Jesus gives us a step by step process to follow which begins with taking our offense to the perpetrator. It is best to confront the problem straight-forwardly and not let it ferment in our hearts. This particular instruction by Jesus is the most difficult teaching to practice. When we do it, we never forget how simple it is.

Moreover, if your brother offends you, go and tell him his fault between you and him alone; if he hears, you have gained your brother. But if he will not hear you, take with you one or two more, that in the mouth of two or three witnesses, every word may be established. And if he neglects to hear them, tell it to the elders...
Matthew 18:15-17

When people hurt us, we assume they knew exactly what they were doing, that they were aware that they hurt us. This assumption is almost always false. People cannot read our minds very well and rarely intentionally hurt us. I have only met one individual in my life who was cruel enough to actually intend to hurt and enjoyed it. But this is a rare individual. We are all well-intentioned beings. We just have trouble communicating and getting our expectations clear in relation to others. Doing what Jesus instructs here builds our character and makes us honest and responsible. We can overcome our lower nature, if we follow this. Acting in accord with Jesus' teachings trains the body to act selflessly and gradually halts our tendencies to indulgence and laziness.

Years ago, when I first began teaching spiritual classes, I had an unusual dream. I found myself in a large outdoor football stadium with the population of the entire world. Thousands upon thousands of people were there, only a very few that I actually knew. All at once, a storm came up, and the whole stadium filled with a brownish-black water. Everyone was sloshing around in this violent sea; some were drowning, some swallowing water, some were struggling to stay afloat. Most were in the process of dying. The waves were so high that I could see the whole stadium from the crest of one. The entire stadium was surrounded by walls of water when the swells rose up around me.

At some point, I remember feeling a great compassion for the others, and with that feeling came a wave which carried me to the side and up over the stadium wall. There, I landed on the richest, most fertile earth I had ever seen. I was on my hands and knees like a child, letting my hands and fingers reach into the soil and feel its warmth. I looked up and saw that I was directly under an orange tree that was ripe with fruit. The sun was shining on this garden, whereas just over the stadium wall, everything was under dark, ominous clouds and experiencing great turbulence. As I sat in the sunny garden, I felt a longing for all of the people struggling and dying in the black soup, and I remember the thought crossing my mind that it would be so easy for them to just swim over to the edge and come into this beautiful garden where I was with my wife and a few others.

This dream symbolized the spiritual path. The stadium was the struggle in the world of attachment, while the garden and the rich fertile soil was the way God had created everything before people contaminated it. My heart was so grateful for the graces which deposited me in the garden, and yet I longed for the others to know what I now knew. Most people are in such a soup, sloshing about and being torn by every wind of fortune. Their lives are out of control, for the most part, and no one is at the helm. Life is determining their fate, because they do not know God, much less what they are doing here on earth. My intuitive feeling at this time is that things will only get worse before people are forced by personal crises to decide to change and build a relationship with God.

When we have exhausted all of the avenues of spiritual expression which seemed interesting to us, we will finally connect with a teacher who has the experience we are seeking. By our own efforts, we may have looked into the various religions, dabbled in the psychic, experimented with various vegetarian diets and meditative techniques. Some peoples' search for God involves a variety of different experiences before they find the path that is meant for them. Others do not seem to need the experience of a long journey or diverse experiences; they just seem to need to wake up to a living practice of the spiritual life in which they are already involved. All these experiences eventually become tedious, by virtue of their not bringing us to the experience of God and our soul.

When we observe people, we see that half of the population is not interested in God, that at their present spiritual development, they are not concerned with a conscious relationship with their Creator. Hunger, jobs, family, finances, and other issues have eclipsed the higher, more spiritual longings of the soul. The other 50% of the population has some degree of longing for God and varying degrees of devotion. It seems to be a perennial condition of human beings that those consciously willing to pay the price to go through the "eye of the needle" are few and far between.

Jesus said it was easier for a camel to go through the eye of the needle than for a rich man to enter into the dominion of heaven. The eye of the needle was an arched passage in one of the twelve gates to Jerusalem which in former times was too low and small for a camel to pass through. The camel had to be unpacked and set on its knees in order to crawl through. When we are rich in opinions, material concerns, desires, or self-pride, we are unable to affect the humility required to enter into the Dominion of God.

Eventually, all souls will return home to our Father. The process may take many painful years of experience, or many lives. The price we have to pay is turning over our little will to the will of God. Letting go of our opinions and rigid ideas about people and life is necessary, in order to see and hear from God's perspective. Our beliefs get us started, but they do not satisfy for long. Only real, spiritual experience brings peace to our souls. Experience is the solid foundation for the rest of our spiritual progress home to God. After return to the Father, we are usually sent forth on missions of service and self-sacrifice, on behalf of the souls who have not awakened as yet.

If knowing God is important to us, we will pray that God send us to a teacher who will instruct us on the way home. All of the things we have done up to this point could have been useful, or they could have been tangents. The disappointment and tedium we feel as we look back at these experiences are indications that we were still trying to do it all ourselves. The final step over the stadium wall can only be given through the help of someone else. Accepting this help requires humility and insures that we will not be permitted to take credit for the blessings in our lives. God is the real teacher; thus, God gets the credit for our successes and accomplishments. God's inspiration guides our thoughts, and in God is the wellspring of our love for others. Nothing is possible without God, if we only had eyes to see.

Find this teacher or instructor, and learn from him or her. Reaching God will take much effort and giving over of personal attachments. It will not be easy or graceful at first. Nothing of any worth is accomplished easily. This is the Great Work which all souls must eventually accomplish. Body, mind, and soul are trained simultaneously in order to bring balance and harmony to the entire human being. The body is disciplined, the mind is controlled, and the soul expands to fill the body, illuminating every part of life with its radiance. The Self is God within the human soul, communicating God's loving guidance as the outer vehicles are purged and cleansed of dross. This process takes time and patience, grace and effort. The things we are asked to do often do not fit into our picture of what would get us closer to God. But the teacher knows from personal experience what brings us to God. We must trust and keep clearly in mind the goal for which we strive.

May you be blessed with the personal blessings of God, as you strive to know and love God. May God guide you to one who will serve as a midwife for your spiritual birth as a son or daughter of God. May you be protected from all evil and the confusion of the world. May you be blessed with the light and peace of Christ, and may you be healed of your past.

꣠

CHAPTER 11
SELF-REALIZATION

"You may rest assured that God sees your struggles, and God will grant you a greater reward for overcoming your selfishness, for holding back a rude word, for satisfying a necessity without being ordered to do so, than if, fighting in a battle, you killed the enemy. The Kingdom of Heaven, which you will possess if you live as just people, is built with the little things of every day. With goodness, moderation, patience, with being satisfied with what one has, bearing with one another, and with love, love, love."

Poem of the Man-God, Maria Valtorta, Volume 2, pg. 229

In 1974, I was sent to Cheyenne, Wyoming, for an unknown amount of time, to train for the ministry. I worked as a welder, sanding welding joints all day to support my family, and then I went to classes and meditations at night. I was not told how long I was to be in Cheyenne, but I had learned that trusting and following the instructions of my teacher was the way to actually come into the experiences that I had heard about and longed to have.

During two different weeks, I was to meditate continually in the chapel at the spiritual center and was placed on silence. No talking. Only meditating and praying. The brothers brought me food, but otherwise I was to be completely with God. When the brothers and sisters came in, I prayed and sang with them, but at all other times, I was silent. I only met with my teacher once a day, to go over what I was learning in meditation and what I was seeing and feeling in my search for God. I was asked to pray to Mother Mary at the Mary shrine, the same shrines we have in all of our Center of Light chapels now. I really loved Mother Mary and was awed by her. But I must say that I did not know how powerful and strong she was, until I spent an hour a day on my knees for a week, praying and really paying attention to her. She was beautiful, pure, and deep beyond words.

One day, I began to feel a burning all over my body. My prayer was to have my misconceptions about the feminine, and women in general, transformed and healed in me. Mary began a dissolution process that was intense and powerful and beyond my conscious ability to anticipate or control. I had asked her to do this, and she was doing it. After a short time of the fire burning all over my body, I fell over. A few minutes later, I was awakened, and I resumed my former kneeling position. One of the brothers in the house was meditating in the chapel at the time, and he probably found this to be quite natural and usual. I was inwardly amused that I had a witness to my loss of control. As I continued, I fainted again under the intensity of the fire.

Later, when I asked my teacher about the incident, he said that I should not try to get away from the pain or the burn but to simply put up with it, endure it, and hang in there with it until it does its job. While I was evacuating from my body, I was actually running away from the change that Mother Mary was trying to accomplish in me. The next day, I readied myself and stayed conscious through the pain of the incineration of the negative energy which I was holding in my cells around the feminine (mothers especially).

Four months later, I was ordained as a minister and empowered to teach classes, serve communion, and do spiritual counseling. I went into meditation, asking to be given the city in which I was to go serve. The answer came: I was to go to San Luis Obispo, California. I left a few weeks later and started a spiritual center in California, as soon as I had gotten a job in a hospital and my daughter was enrolled in school.

After a year on mission, teaching and gathering together about thirty students and moving them along the spiritual path, I was back in Cheyenne for a seminar. During this time, many students were coming into the Illumination, really taking on the teachings and moving through many transformative changes. At the seminar, Master Marthelia, one of the teachers of the Holy Order of Mans (HOOM), brought me into Self-Realization. This spiritual initiation brings one into the experience of seeing God and the soul at the center of one's being. It was an ecstasy and an embrace, where God greeted me, and I met God with an open heart.

God has known us since we were created, but near the time of Self-Realization, the creature, the human being, has done the work of getting him or herself out of the way. A person has to really go within in meditation, keeping her mind still to the point where she is introduced to the Father God who created her. I was noticeably different the day following my passage through Self-Realization; I was in a deep state of peace that was beyond all description. I was filled with a recognition that I am in the right place, on the right planet, and completely loved. Few descriptions could come close to conveying to you what it is like using mere words.

After this experience, I was not in any fear of death. I could not imagine what I was thinking to have been so separate from God up until that point, or to have thought anything meaningful was outside of me. All the most beautiful love in the Universe was inside my chest. The Kingdom of Heaven was within me, and I was invited into its gates. I was able to hear God speak to me, and I could speak to God in return, and we embraced for what felt like the first time. Although I do know my soul remembers having been this close to God before, in other lifetimes of service to God.

Father Paul Blighton, the founder and original director of the Holy Order of Mans, was an engineer by trade, dedicated to discerning and teaching the scientific and spiritual truths of the Universe.

The process for students as they progress along the inner path is that, sometime after they have the light of Christ sealed in their flesh during the Illumination, the teacher will ask them to look within for the source of that light. This is often an arduous process, but it does not have to take terribly long. Each person has his or her own set of resistances and concepts that get in the way of moving inside to the soul and Self. I was watched over by my teacher to see when this gift of Self-Realization could safely be given to me. I was not aware of whether I was ready, nor did I have any idea how to evaluate that. That is the teacher's job. Only one who has that much humility and has been appropriately trained is able or allowed to administer such an initiation for a disciple. Every true and real teacher is under loving obedience to God, or he or she is a false teacher.

Only one who has gone through this initiation could possibly imagine the amount of gratitude one has to God and the immense appreciation for the instrument of the teacher through which this is done. All of the teachings are fulfilled in this incredible experience, and one is not the same anymore. One has graduated from being merely human and has entered into the first stages of being a son or daughter of God. I have often said that this is the graduation from the animal-human status to full human being status.

After my Self-Realization in Wyoming, I went back to California and continued having many experiences in teaching and training people. I formed four spiritual communities of disciples, two in Indiana and two in California, and I taught and prepared many students for the Illumination. In 1979, I became disillusioned by the HOOM and the ones who had taken over the running of that order. I was a minister, and my striving and intention was to become a priest, if it was God's will. I had been told inside by God that I would be a priest, so I was certain that the Holy Order of Mans was the avenue through which I would be ordained. I never even questioned that conclusion. Then the HOOM began to pull back because of the Jim Jones disaster, as a public scare about cults developed, and the Order stopped opening up to the public to teach classes anymore. The teachers also stopped bringing people into the initiation of Illumination.

To me, these looked like signs of change which were not for the best. To confirm my intuition, there was some talk of turning to orthodoxy, such as the patriarchal fathers of the early Russian or Greek Orthodox churches. Master Andrew was running the order at this time. He had been trained by Father Paul, the original founder and director of the HOOM, and he was the third teacher to run the HOOM after Father Paul had died.

It had been in April 1974 – on Good Friday – that Father Paul Blighton, the founder and original director of the HOOM, had died. At the time, he was replaced by Master Raeson Ruiz as the director of the HOOM. Master Raeson directed the HOOM for a year. Raeson had had the idea that the three teachers of the HOOM would each run the order for a year. At the end of three years, one of them would have come to a sufficiently deep understanding of the job and the responsibilities of the work, and the other two would then be supportive of whoever would finally take the Director job on for life.

The third teacher to run the HOOM was Andrew Rossi. Apparently, Rossi had a secret and lingering desire to be recognized by an orthodox tradition, a desire which began to reveal itself. Rossi was the one at the helm as the ship of the HOOM slowly sunk. His leadership had contributed to the HOOM's demise, rather than saving it. All the women priests of the HOOM went back to domestic duties and child rearing, whereas before they were dynamic priests and servants of God. All of the transformative teaching and preparation for initiations was removed and no longer a part of the HOOM's work.

In 1979, as the HOOM was sinking, I wrote a couple of letters to Andrew Rossi requesting further training, because even though I was a minister, I was not an ordained priest. After being Self-Realized, I was clearly on track for the priesthood. On both occasions, he rebuffed my correspondence. Not giving up, I drove from Indiana, where I was living at the time, out to California on my motorcycle. While there attending a Gestalt Therapy conference, I contacted Master Andrew for an interview in person. His secretary said he was busy for two months straight through.

When I called the next day to speak to him, I had to tell his staff that I was available any twenty-minute segment of any day or night for a week. If he could arrange to meet me anywhere, I would be available. The response I received was that he was unable to do that for two months. I was angry and hurt, and I told the brother who spoke for him that even God was more available than he was. I went into sadness and somewhat of a despair, because now the realization hit me: I might not become a priest this lifetime. I was also painfully aware that the door to the HOOM had just closed for me permanently. I was sure God wanted me to be a priest, and now the only avenue I knew of for that to happen was closed. I knew I was completely finished with the HOOM, and so I drove my motorcycle up to Yellowstone National Park. I sat out in the rain all day in the woods with the bears, to pray and try to get some inner guidance on what to do.

At that point, I was not really concerned with my life, because it was as if my life was finished. I was not worried about whether a grizzly attacked and ate me, because everything had seemed to close up around me, and I felt completely alone. I tried to get inner guidance from God all day, but I could not hear a thing. God was allowing me to get completely immersed in the temptation to despair. Would I continue to have faith, or would I go into a permanent depression? I was quite broken and hurt by the door of my concepts closing in my face. The HOOM was not the avenue through which I would be ordained and further trained.

That evening, I laid my head down on the pillow, as I had checked into a motel. I asked God one more time what I was supposed to do. God said very simply, "Be a priest." When I asked how, God said to go home and start to teach classes again, whether there was an order or not. I asked, "What about the Sacraments and the Initiations?," because I knew that, without being a priest, I could not administer the blessings.. God told me God would take care of that, that I could still baptize people and give a blessed but not transmuted Communion. Exhausted and excited, I rested contented and felt deeply loved. I traveled home hastily and began to teach the next week.

A class gathered quickly, and within a year, I had another thirty students who were moving along and growing, becoming light-filled disciples of Jesus and his Mother Mary. About this time, a couple of my students visited relatives in Detroit, Michigan, a relatively short trip from where I was living, working, and teaching in Bloomington, Indiana. It was in Detroit that my students made connection with Master Raeson Ruiz, who had recently left the HOOM and was teaching and working as a drug rehab counselor. He was holding some classes, and my students informed me of this. I was not impressed, because I reasoned that if he had left the HOOM, he was probably wounded and not functioning much as a true teacher anymore.

A few weeks later, he called me and asked why I was saying bad things about him. I admitted it and said that I thought he could not be doing too well. He asked me to not form judgments unless I had talked to him first. I apologized, and as we talked, he said he would like to come to Bloomington to teach a priest class to me and some of my best students. I was floored and overwhelmed. This was truly a surprise. Never in my wildest dreams would I have thought this would be possible. A few months later, he moved down to Indiana and started teaching a group of eight of us.

Master Raeson was in his fifties and had grown up on the streets of New York as a Puerto Rican youth. He was street-wise, but he was very loving and awake. Many people thought him a little austere, because he looked like a Zen monk, with a shaved head and a penetrating gaze. He could size you up in minutes and then disarm you with something very loving and warm. He was also very pointed when he needed to be, saying things that were necessary but sometimes hard to hear, and thus he inspired a lot of respect and, in some of my students, some caution and anxiety.

He trained eight priests and ordained them one by one. He waited to ordain me last, which caused a tremendous jostling of the egos of the whole class. My former students thought they were much further along than I was because they were ordained before me. Master Raeson was the kind of person who would let people think what they wanted to, and then surprise them and see how they would change or react from the experience. So on the last day for ordinations, I was ordained with a back-to-back ordination: first as a priest and then as a Master Teacher. It was April 11, 1982, eight years after I first had been ordained a minister. None of the class knew I would be ordained as a Master Teacher, so they were quite shocked when it happened.

Master Raeson Ruiz, one of three remaining teachers after the demise of the Holy Order of Mans, trained and ordained Father Peter as a Priest and Master Teacher, also passing on the Rites of Ordination to him.

Since they had thought they were more advanced because of being ordained sooner, now that I was ordained in a supervisory capacity for them as priests, they were not happy. Unfortunately, they had not let go of some of the more obvious character flaws in their personality. This was the shock value that Master Raeson was looking for, and it did a nice job of weeding out a few of them early on by causing them to withdraw. Very few of their egos could stand me being over them spiritually after they had felt so above me for months. In fact, all but one of them left permanently within about four months.

About this time, Master Raeson moved into my house with my family and taught me personally for ten months. We served Communion daily and meditated together and spent most of my non-work time together. It was during this time that I owned and managed the restaurant in Bloomington to put me through graduate school. So when I was not at work, I was at home with my wife and my daughter and Master Raeson. Master Raeson was as an older brother to me, and he taught me everything he knew. During this time, I learned that he was ailing and was on some kind of special diet that he would not really explain to anyone. It seemed to be a bad situation; I could feel he was aware of something ominous coming down in his life. I was saddened by the prospect of losing him. But each day, we continued to talk about the HOOM and his experiences with Father Paul Blighton, his teacher.

He told me that just before Father Paul died, he asked Master Raeson secretly to fly home to the ranch in Sebastopol, California, to meditate in the chapel there. Father Paul seemed to be aware that he was going to pass through transition. Master Raeson reported that, while he was in the chapel meditating, he felt such a weight of responsibility resting on his shoulders that he could hardly kneel up or sit on a chair. He could barely lay his head up on the kneeler at the Mary shrine. He was being given the spiritual responsibility of the HOOM and Father Paul's responsibility as a Master Teacher.

Father Peter pictured with Master Raeson on April 11th, 1982, the day of his ordination into the Priesthood and spiritual Mastery

The prospect was overwhelming and intense. Master Raeson revealed to me that he knew he had been selected to be the one to take over the HOOM, but that, because he was not well-liked by the two other Teachers, Philip and Andrew, he would have a hard time taking on the job without their support. This was when he decided to take the lead the first year and agree to each of them leading the next two years. His idea was that, at the end of three years, the other two Teachers would realize Master Raeson should be the one to take over permanently and would be supportive of him leading the HOOM. Though the idea was good, it did not turn out as he planned. When Andrew Rossi took over, he ousted Master Raeson for some silly rule he dreamed up, and Raeson left.

What I came to realize was that Master Raeson was the one who had been given Father Paul's mission to continue, and he was preparing me to do that when he left. But here he was dying and not talking about it. One morning during Communion, I was serving Master Raeson, and he leaned back on his haunches and began to weep. I was aware of the cause of his tears, but I was too respectful to mention it. When we came out of the chapel, he asked what I saw. I told him that I was not comfortable telling him what I saw, since he saw it too. It was not for me to say. He told me he wanted me to tell him. So we sat down, and I reluctantly told him that God told me he should go to the woods and meditate and just leave his body there, like the wise old Indian Chiefs do when they know it is their time to pass over. He was also aware that this was what he was being told, and he wept some more. I was so sad. I knew it was right, but it was going to take courage. So he resolved to pack up, and in a couple of days, he began to do just that.

A few months before this time, he and I had gone to Kansas City to begin teaching a priest class there. That was the last time he went with me to Kansas City or Ocean City, New Jersey, where another priest class was being taught. We had planned to take turns teaching these classes, but he was too ill to come with me. Master Raeson had given me Rites of Ordination in September of 1982, which gave me the authority to ordain priests and teachers. But I was without any students at that time. Because, of course, after I was ordained a Master Teacher, all of the students had left within a few months. So I had had to start all over, drawing new students, in the summer of 1982. It was in the spring of 1983 that Master Raeson left for the woods to die.

A couple weeks after he supposedly went out to leave his body in the woods, he showed up in my driveway, waiting for me when I drove in. He was not looking well. His brain tumor was starting to take him down, and he was getting a little funny in the head. He was not thinking straight, and he was ripping up his teacher robe over my trash can. The tumor had apparently interfered with his volition and his ability to follow the guidance to leave his body out in the woods. I knew his brain was going. He was only 52 years old. I told him he had to get some help and he could not stay with me any longer. He agreed and left, to have his wife take him to a hospital in Indianapolis. He died in the hospital a couple of months later.

After his death, I took on the responsibility of continuing the priest classes in Kansas City and Ocean City. I was in my fourth year of a doctoral program in Educational Psychology at Indiana University, was running a fledgling spiritual order, and was a full-time manager and owner of a successful restaurant. All of that together was not nothing. I was very busy, to say the least. I was also managing a family life. My second daughter had been born on the birthday of the Brotherhood of Christ, on November 26, 1982. My wife was also teaching and helping in the restaurant. But the weight of things was on me, and I took it seriously. The Brotherhood of Christ grew and we were teaching much the same as the HOOM, except we had a whole wealth of psychological training and awareness that the HOOM teachers did not have and therefore could not use.

Through it all, I never doubted the power of Jesus and Mary to make things happen or to make the new order successful. But sometimes I was not so sure we were going to draw people to us who would help us with the task.

In 1983, I met Linda Watts,who had some training in the HOOM and was living in Kentucky. She was practicing as a midwife and traveled to Bloomington to attend my classes every month. I ordained her a deaconaround this time and she started teaching classes in Kentucky, gathering students at her home. She was the kind of person who was initially serious and somewhat intense in her energy, but she was very willing to get to work and help. She was very busy with four kids and a large midwifery practice, able to take a lot of work on without a lot of supervision. Then, in 1985, she moved to Boston with her family and began to work with one of my students whom I ordained as a teacher in the Brotherhood of Christ, who left shortly afterward.

Meanwhile, I graduated from Indiana University with a Doctorate in Educational Psychology in May, 1984. After that, I moved with my family to Milwaukee, Wisconsin, to find a job in psychology. But jobs were tough to find. So I worked as a Systems Analyst for a manufacturing firm for a year, running their computer system. This was definitely not my kind of work, even though I managed all right with the job. I had sold the restaurant for ten times what I initially put into it, and thus we were able to live on that money the first year out of school. About ten of our students from Indiana moved to Milwaukee with us and got their own homes and jobs to support themselves. We continued classes and Communion Services in our new home and began to draw students from the city.

Father Peter pictured with his second and youngest daughter Carin, in Milwaukee, Wisconsin

The Brotherhood of Christ grew over the next few years. We now had centers in Boston, Springfield, Philadelphia, Kansas City, and Ocean City, New Jersey, in addition to Milwaukee. But the members did not grow very much and, as in some organizations, they seemed only too willing for the leaders to be doing all the work. This contributed to the eventual demise of the Brotherhood of Christ. The Order had started to get somewhat inbred, with no new blood or new students being drawn. Some of the priests and ministers seemed embroiled in their own problems, and the outlook was seemingly a bit dismal.

During this time, I started a psychotherapy practice, seeing clients and building a clientele. In addition, I taught two classes a semester in Educational Psychology, at the

University of Wisconsin-Milwaukee, for a period of nine years, from 1984 to 1993. In 1985, I began a remodeling contracting business, since I was not making enough to support two kids and a family on what little I was making at the time. I worked two jobs essentially for about eight years, while I was raising two daughters, building a practice, and running a spiritual order. Those years took their toll on my marriage.

My oldest daughter was troubled and had an attitude problem that was well over a mile wide. She stayed out late at night or would not come home at all. It took months for me to learn to not stay awake after hearing the screen door opened. Even though it made no sound at all, I felt the energy of the house change when the door opened, and then I was wide awake. I had to train myself to not wake up when she came in at all hours of the night. My wife had differing ideas on discipline, which provided an easy out for my daughter to take liberties.

With all the stress from working many jobs, the lack of growth in the Brotherhood of Christ, and the strains in the marriage, things were coming to a head. I took the family to Italy and to Medjugorie, Yugoslavia, in January of 1989. I had heard about six teenagers in Yugoslavia who were visited by Mother Mary each night. They had been given messages about the inevitable calamities predicted for the earth if people did not pray. Millions of people made pilgrimages to Medjugorie, to obtain graces and healings and blessings from Mother Mary. Many miracles and changes resulted for people. The appearances of Mother Mary in Fatima and Lourdes years earlier had inspired me to make sure I did not miss out on this experience. Also, I thought my daughters would be blessed by the experience and would come away moved and changed.

It was a moving experience, when we felt Mother Mary as she appeared to the six teenage children. We met the kids and talked to them. We felt Mary come each night, when she entered the little church to give revelations to the kids. We were traveling with a couple of student Catholic priests from Rome. One of the priests had purchased two silver-chained rosaries outside the Vatican, from a street vendor. He gave them to one of the Franciscan friars to bless when he arrived.

The friar gave them back to him the next day, and one of them had turned into a gold-chained rosary. The priest who had bought them took them into Mostar to have a jeweler test them the next day. It was verified: the rosary had turned from silver into 18th century, 18-carat gold. That was the rosary the student priest had acquired to give to his mother. He was, of course, amazed. I was not that amazed at such miracles or healings, as I had witnessed many such miracles happing during my many years in the ministry. From my own experience, I knew Mother Mary was very powerful, and her presence was very strong in that little village.

When we got back to Rome, I received in meditation from Jesus to disband the Brotherhood of Christ, since it was not growing and had mostly atrophied. I told the membership when I got home. They were very upset and disillusioned. Some became angry, and some were in shock. I advised them to find a church or a spiritual practice, even the Catholic Church, to receive Communion. Some were so hurt and angry that they turned against me. But I was not concerned with their reactions, as I knew I was being obedient. My wife was pleased at the disbanding of the Brotherhood, because she did not want to teach or be a minister anymore. She just wanted to take care of the kids and get her Master's degree in Counseling. We were not getting along very well at this time, and it was affecting the kids. We both focused on getting our Jungian training and developing our psychotherapy practices. We attended several rounds of couples counseling and individual counseling, which helped a little, but those efforts did not resolve some deep-seated differences.

For the first ten months after the closure of the Brotherhood, I joined with some of the former Brotherhood members at the 6:00 a.m. Communion in the Catholic Church. Each day, we prayed the Rosary, asking with the dedication to pray for the end of the Iran–Iraq war. In eight months, the war ended, and a month or two later the Berlin wall was taken down. We felt like we had definitely helped to make those prayers of thousands of people come true. Prayer works. I am not so presumptuous as to believe that we were the only ones praying for this war to end. But we knew we had helped. I started to teach again without the formal backdrop of an Order, and some of the former students attended. I simply could not stop teaching, even though the Brotherhood was gone. I taught a couple of students through the next four or five years. My psychotherapy practice was growing, and I was helping people interpret their dreams and visions. Since I had a spiritual component to my practice, people were growing in consciousness there too.

My oldest daughter went to the music conservatory at Lawrence University in 1990, for a voice degree. This helped ease some of the tension in our home, but it was also difficult for her mom, who by now had become depressed. But life goes on, and we moved on as best we could, having apparently scarred each other irreparably. When 1996 came around, my second daughter was in violin training, and her mom was focused totally on stage mothering. The tension in the family was very high. I longed to teach more formally again but was trying not to speak of it, as it was not a popular subject in the family.

In 1996, Linda Watts called from Boston with a dream that I was to ordain her as a priest. I had been in contact with her every few months since the Brotherhood disbanded, and my wife was not happy with these conversations. She imagined I was having affairs, which was never the case. I flew with my wife to Boston to ordain Linda, later called Clare, as a priest in November, 1996. My wife barely tolerated the experience and was now more negative about any teaching relationships that I had. When students or clients called the house, she was decidedly negative.

Father Peter with Reverend Clare in the early days of their ministry together

I started teaching classes again in 1997 without pointing out to the students that I was a priest or teacher. It seemed appropriate to let them realize what energy and consciousness was working through me without having any titles or outward show of my ordinations. I could have been fine with my wife doing her own thing and me doing mine,

194

if she had been positive and not negative about my relationship with students. But she was negative and entirely unsupportive. I learned many years later that she had told my daughters for years that I was having affairs with the women students who were calling. In fact, there was never any affair during the entire thirty years of our marriage.

It was in 1997 that I began experiencing stress symptoms in the form of ringing in my ears, accompanied by nausea spells and vomiting, during which I could not function for a couple of days at a time. I was losing my therapy clients because I had to reschedule so much. Finally, I realized that my marriage was not working. When I asked God what to do, I was told the relationship was over and that I needed to move out. I left the house immediately. Right away, my symptoms cleared up, and I felt better. I began to teach more seriously and gathered a group of students.

Reverend Clare was teaching in Boston and was focusing on drawing women students. But she was now having some men come to her classes, and I was having mostly women come. So we decided to travel to each other's centers and team-teach. This worked very well. Since we were administering the same teachings and the same process of training, we decided to form the Order of Christ Sophia together. On April 15th, 1999, this new Order was incorporated. We started with two Centers of Light: one in Boston and one in Milwaukee. We began to train people who were serious about their spiritual life and were willing to work toward an experience of God, instead of merely believing or buying into some dogma. 199

ॐ

CHAPTER 12
THE RADICAL PATH

How difficult it is for a rich person to enter the Dominion of Heaven, the gate of which is narrow and the way of which is steep, and those who are laden with the bulky weights of riches cannot go along it and enter. To enter up there, only the immaterial treasures of virtue are required, and one must be able to part with everything that is an attachment to the things of the world and to vanity.

Poem of The Man-God, Maria Valtorta, Volume 5, pg. 288

The hardest thing you will ever do is give up the tendency to try to control everything. If you are at all interested in the spiritual life, you may have a whole set of reasons for finding it fascinating. You may be disgusted with your life. You may have seen past all the superficial rewards for living a completely unexamined existence. You might be one of those who are really done with inconsequential things, trivial indulgences, and meaningless relationships. You might be certain that there is much more to life than you have experienced, searching far and long to enter into some of the experiences about which the mystics and saints have written. If you feel that your life has been a series of misdirected searches and over-anxious accomplishments, then you might want to consider something radical.

If you have exhausted your personal ability to make sense of life and have tried many things in the hopes of understanding the meaning of life, then maybe you are ready for something revolutionary, something transforming in your life. The spiritual path is a departure from the way the world teaches and the fulfillment the mass consciousness offers. A true spiritual path will set you at odds with the way the majority of people think, feel, and act.

If you follow what the world teaches, you are certain to be miserable, lonely, afraid, anxious, and confused. The world says that everything you see is the way it really is. The mass consciousness declares that only what is tangible is real, and that only what will make you a distinct individual, unique and original, will get you love. With vast numbers of people doing the very same things, people become less and less themselves. By trying to be different and clever, you merely create a reaction to others that you have to maintain in all relationships. That makes you stressed out – and more and more out of touch with your inner nature. Going further into what the world suggests will get you further from the truth of your inner being. Remember, you are wearing a body, but you are not that body. You have acquired earthly traits, but most of those traits are not who you really are. The spiritual path is a complete turnaround from what you have been focusing on and how the world thinks.

As Jesus said, "Narrow is the way that leads to life, and there will be few who go in that way, while broad is the way and wide is the gate that leads to destruction, and many will go in that way." It is a narrow, difficult road to turn away from the patterns and acceptances of the world to follow the inner path. Jesus also stated that he was going to set a person at variance against those of his or her own family. This means that most of the acceptances family and friends have will have to be examined and evaluated to see if they are consistent with the spiritual life. Most of the traditions of the family are designed to preserve the status quo and keep everyone in their place.

Life in the family should have been a school, where God was represented by the example of the parents. Parents should have stood in for God, in the way they taught, trained, and supported a child as a soul. But with the majority of people not even knowing they have a soul, and millions less ever actually seeing and knowing their own souls, how can parents teach their children about the soul, much less see them as souls? Most children are considered appendages of the parents, owned and manipulated by them as extensions of themselves. That is blatantly false, and it is a complete violation of them as souls who have God inside. The statement made by Jesus, "I have not come to bring peace on earth, but a sword," was not simply to make things difficult. It was a statement of fact, that moving onto the Spiritual Path is a radical departure from the way the world thinks. As Jesus said, very few will go in the narrow gate, while many will go into destruction through the wide gate.

Family traditions, patterns of the mass mind, what the world expects and considers important – all are opposed to the process of spiritual development. For those of you who are pretty well disillusioned by what the world offers in terms of enjoyments, lusts, power, addictions, and failed relationships, you might want to be thinking of an alternative to a vacuous life. The Radical Path is just such an alternative. But the Radical Path will set you apart from other people. That might scare some of you who are craving or even begging for people to love you. You might want to admit that you have been falling short in the discrimination department, considering those who you have wanted to love you. That is because you have been and maybe still are so desperate for someone out there to really care about you.

But the word "holy" means "set apart," and if you are gradually becoming a holy person, then you will not be able to think like others, and that will set you apart. You will express love where others express negative emotions. You will see past appearances while others react to what they see on the surface. You will feel loved from God inside, while others are begging, manipulating, and hurting other people, stealing love from outside them. The Radical Path will make you look in the mirror and see those things in yourself that are absolutely no good for you. You will start to feel disenchanted with what you used to find enjoyable. The Radical Path will give you spiritual sight, to see past the appearances of things to what is really going on. Your spiritual sight will open as you let those teaching you bring you into a whole new life and a whole new world of reality.

What is radical about the spiritual path? Looking within instead of outside of your for answers is revolutionary. Inside you is the reality of God's Being, the part of you that shines brightly with luminous light. From the center of your being, God lives and radiates, waiting for you to let yourself be loved. Looking inside is precisely opposite the direction in which most people look when trying to discover who they are. They look outside themselves, rather, to all the ways people are striving to be different, and they adopt some combination of elements taken from the culture or the media. Then, they strive after those outer trappings, hoping to find happiness and fulfillment. They go through round after round of striving and fruitless attempts at attaining, until a hopeless feeling arises in their psyche.

On the spiritual path, one has a teacher. Having a teacher seems so dependent, so weak and immature, from the world view. But from God's perspective, God wants each person to be personally taught by God, the Being who created us. Having a teacher is a natural part of creation, since God originally set it up that our parents would be our first teachers. Too often, these parents fail to really embody what God would be like, if God were functioning through human parents. Parents were supposed to stand in for God for 20 short years, until the young adult would be launched into the world and make his or her own way in life. But instead, what people mostly receive is incredible imperfection, and sometimes even meanness and selfishness, as the day-to-day example from their caregivers.

I know it is obvious to most of you how little love you received as a child. By now, that is old news. But the damage from this reality is not old news. The repetition of those patterns learned in early life are lived out, over and over, in every relationship, many times throughout your life. The healing of those patterns can only come in a direct relationship with God, through a personal connection with a human teacher.

I am not talking about someone professing to be a teacher. I am talking about someone who has humbly submitted to being taught by his or her spiritual teacher, until that teacher considers him or her to be developed enough to be in a position to teach other people. Usually, the main criterion for someone to receive that benediction is a good, strong, honest love for other people. Possessing such a love sets a person apart from his or her brothers and sisters. This love is one in which a person has learned to love others as he or she loves him or herself. Many people want to be honored. Many want to be respected. Many do not even mind being feared. But how many truly know how to love without thinking about themselves and their needs being met?

This may not seem so radical to you yet. Maybe it is, maybe it is not. But I will tell you more. You will have to eventually let go of controlling your process. You will have to allow someone else to love you enough to lead you into the experience of God. You will not be able to control that. Most of the time, you will not even be able to know what the next step is. You will not be able to preview the experience, knowing what is next, because you have not been there yet. You will not be permitted to make God your little pet, or your little toy employee. God is much, much bigger than you can ever conceive, and God will not have any other gods before God. So everything which God has not built, everything to which God does not give God's blessing, will be taken apart and dismantled. Nothing will be left of the false creations or the distorted desires. God will run this spiritual show – not you.

For some, that means a kind of inner death, where your ego cannot take credit for everything anymore. Some people will be disappointed with the spiritual process and, because of their pride, will run away and try to do what they had been doing before – orchestrate everything themselves. They will fall away from the spiritual life, because they are still in fear and have not been introduced to perfect love yet. How can you want a relationship with God, and then demand that God conform to your schedule, your way, your idiosyncrasies and your style? You are a created being; you are not the Creator. That should give you pause when you are trying to grow yourself spiritually.

The fact is, you cannot guide yourself. If you could, you would have. You would already have gotten yourself to the peace, light, and love within, because of course, why would you choose anything less for yourself? You are drawn by God to the spiritual life, as God wishes every one of God's creations to be in blissful union with God. Most people have actually willed themselves into separation and need a major healing to get back into connection with God. The Radical Path provides that healing and transformation.

It is radical to leave the mind of the world. It is radical to set limits with the parents and family members who continuously try to manipulate you to stay in the box in which they imagine you. It is revolutionary to go inside yourself to the Divine Source within and commune there. In that communion, you are brought into balance and loved like it could never be possible in any human relationship. If you think you have had that experience with a human being, then you are blessed. But if you think that that human experience is comparable to the ecstatic embrace with God, then you have not had that blessing of union with God, or you could never say that. You might be able to

202

partially describe the experience, but you cannot imagine it until you have it.

The Radical Spiritual Path takes you into a place where you do not see the same way anymore. You do not use the same eyes that others use. You see with your spiritual senses opened, and so you see past what appears immediately, to that which is behind facades. You start to see energy and motives and inner, secret things. You start to smell illness and fear and pride. You become acutely aware when someone is speaking with the voice of darkness, or when someone is trying to get you to follow a voice that is not God. You become more and more transformed and healed by your meditations, your receiving of daily Communion, and by the classes that are being taught and the blessings given. You whole life is becoming God-centered and God-blessed.

You might fear that, should you pursue this life of which I speak, should you strive to become "holy," you will no longer have any fun. This fear is common. You fear that you will never have those enjoyments of by-gone days, as you enter into more and more of a holy, sacred life. But the bliss and joy of being with God is so much greater than those past mere glimpses, you finally just give all and enter into God, with a true dedication to serve and be one with God. You lose your attachments to the earth and to your former life, as you make your way through the outer death to the inner life.

For those of you that have fully chosen this Radical Spiritual Path, it becomes increasingly obvious that there is nothing more important and that you would easily die for the life you are being shown. When you have given over into the radical life, nothing is hard anymore. Nothing is too much for you. You do not shy away from confrontations or difficulties. You do not fear your own death or any insults to your person. Instead, you know that these things are a part of living a holy life, and they are a mark that God has blessed you. You do not have any more "martyred" tendencies, because you know you are loved. You merely want to give back those things you have been given, as you were lovingly taught and trained from the beginning of your spiritual path.

One of the greatest joys of the spiritual life is seeing students really taking on the spiritual life after having been healed of many things. They start to become who they were created to be, and their God qualities emerge in the process of their unfoldment. They let go of their fear and pride and allow God to move in them, causing a transformation of their whole person. There is nothing more joyful than to be part of that process, and to share in that with a new son or daughter of God.

If you want to be different from the way the world is, believe in God. Seek to discover God at the center of your being. Open to be taught by a true teacher, one so designated by their teacher. Let the love move in you, until you open completely to their love. If you want to really grow, then let go of the old ways. Let go of the way you have tried to distinguish yourself, and find out who you really are. Give up all your attachments.

Let go of toxic relationships to parents, family, and friends, and set limits with them on how you allow them to treat you. If they do not respect you, then try to speak to them about it and get them to treat you differently. If they do not stop treating you as little or manipulating you in the old ways, then inform them that you will have to be more distant from them. If they do not want that, then they will change or stop. If they will not change or stop, then you have to be firm and cut them off. It is simple. Stop imagining that you have to have toxic people in your life. You owe them nothing. Parents were supposed to have given you a body out of love for you. Was it love, or did they think you owed them for their sacrifice?

Also, let go of the ways you have tried to squeeze joy out of life. Those thrills and enjoyments did not satisfy, or you would have been satiated and fulfilled by them. You still crave them because they were not satisfying. At the back of all of those addictive energies is a desire for someone to love you and take care of you. That means you did not get that experience growing up. Now, the only way to really get that love and fulfillment is in a relationship with God. Let the rest go.

ᘓ

CHAPTER 14
BUILDING AN ORDER

When I will have taken you to my Father, through me, and you have been cleansed and strengthened by my blood and sorrow, grace will come back to you, lively and powerful, and you will be triumphant, if you so wish. God does no violence to your thoughts or your sanctification. You are free. But God gives you back your strength. God gives you back your freedom from Satan's empire. It depends on you, with me as your brother to guide you and nourish you with an immortal food.

Poem of the Man-God, Maria Valtorta, Volume 2, pg. 135

The first thing Reverend Clare and I had to decideon as we began our order was what materials to use to teach the students. I suggested the Tree of Life lessons, which had been the avenue through which I was taught. She asked me to rewrite them so they were more readable and de-gendered. I volunteered to rewrite them, improving them and making them more accessible and usable. The following three weeks, I worked on completely overhauling them, until they were in much better shape. And so we started using those lessons as our tool for teaching the mysteries.

We then went through everything else that the former HOOM had used to train and teach people, and I rewrote virtually everything. It was a huge job, but it was necessary. Through our process in developing our own teachings, we discovered that the way the HOOM people had been taught was not thorough, in that it did not actually transform in them the deep-seated problems with which they first came. It became extremely clear to us that the psychological component of the inner work was necessary, if people were going to be able to address the emotional issues that were holding them back. One can teach the spiritual teachings and a person can adopt them, but that person might still be riddled with anger and fears and childhood wounds that plague him or her throughout his or her ministry.

Also, we saw how those former members of the HOOM that we encountered were the walking wounded, in that they had not overcome their original fears and anger stemming from their family history. That meant that they had not received help seeing those problems and overcoming and healing them. I recalled the HOOM members being so insulated even when they were together, as if everyone was out for his or her own spiritual development. They did not feel like brothers and sisters in a loving family. They felt like benevolent competitors hoping to advance past each other, to be better than the others. That felt completely wrong to me.

We worked on ways to make sure that this did not happen in our order. We devised methods for getting to those difficult areas and healing them. We also stayed away from the emphasis on criticism and power, and focused more on training, teaching, and loving students into their healing. We de-gendered the teachings and reorganized the structure of how the Order of Christ Sophia (OCS) would support its work. We decided on the basic tithing method used in the churches. We also made a discrimination that was very important: that people had to have their material world tasks taken care of in order to be ready for spiritual training. This meant that people had to be self-supporting, having a career and an income stream, and having a place to live, in order to be ready to do the spiritual work. If they did not have the material world tasks together, we understood that they were still working on getting those skills or were actively acting out anger at their parents.

For the first few years of the OCS, Mother Clare and I taught weekend seminars together in the two cities in which we had Centers, alternating lectures. Then, when we started two new centers in 2001, this set-up became unwieldy. We realized that it was more efficient to have us both teaching simultaneously at two Centers of Light, rather than teaching at only one at a time, with both of us present. If we split up, we could serve two Centers on the same weekend. Also, we were looking into the future and could see that we would be opening many Centers down the road. We knew we would have to spread our work around efficiently in order for the Centers to see a Master Teacher as often as possible.

In the first expansion of the order beyond the original two Centers of Light in Milwaukee and Boston, Mother Clare moved to Seattle to open a new center, and I moved to Oakland, California, to do the same. By then, we had grown enough to have trained priests take charge of running the two original centers. We were growing and expanding and learning how to really bring people along spiritually. Each of the centers was attracting students who were at varying stages of spiritual development. This warranted the opening of priest and deacon classes that were taught on seminar weekends. As students moved into ministry training for the priesthood, we developed an apprenticeship model, where more experienced priests supervised and counseled the newer priests. The newer priests had to sit in and observe the more seasoned priests teaching and counseling, in order to gain experience in how to serve in this way.

When I had been helping Mother Clare move from Boston to Seattle in August of 2001, I fell off the UHaul ramp and broke my left wrist. The break was quite severe; I had to have surgery to install ten pins, nuts, and bolts in my wrist. They even had to implant some coral from the ocean, in order to add calcium and bone for the healing. After the surgery, I was supposed to be left with 60% of my left wrist and hand function. But the surgeons were superb and were using a new experimental surgery. With the help of some of the occupational therapists within OCS, I began regaining the function of my wrist. In the past, I had played guitar occasionally. Now, I thought I might never be able to play again. When I held the guitar, I could barely press down the strings. But then, being a practical sort, I decided to try to play some cords and use that as exercise for my wrist. Soon, I had gained some function back, and I was actually able to play.

About this time, immediately after I ordained Mother Clare as a master teacher, she came out of seclusion and was pretty adamant and forceful that I should be writing spiritual songs as she remembered me doing that in another lifetime. She had made negative comments about the fact that I would only play folk-rock songs by the likes of James Taylor, the Beatles, and Bob Dylan. So in September of 2001, I wrote a song to Mother Mary. The music was moving for the students. This strengthened my resolve to write a few more, and in a couple of months, I had twelve songs. One of our student's husbands was a recording engineer, and he offered (or rather she offered) his services to help with recording the songs.

Because I had never recorded anything, I did not even know what a studio looked like on the inside. There we were, a bunch of priests dressed in funny clothes (blacks and clerical collars), storming Dave Locke's studio to record thirteen songs about Jesus and Mary. In two days, we finished the album, and we were happy with it. The album actually turned out very good, considering we knew nothing about recording and were such amateurs. This first CD was entitled *Devoted To You* and became available in the winter of 2002. Since then, I have written over 200 songs and, at the time of this printing, have produced 18 albums.

We started to gather all of the members together twice a year, at Summer and Winter Retreats. At these Retreats, all the students, ministers, and priests came to learn and grow together. Our Retreats were and have always remained intense, not sleepy. People go through intense changes at retreats, and they learn a tremendous amount about themselves, God, Jesus, and Mary. The Master Teachers give the lectures, and the conversations at meals are substantive and real, not superficial or light. Members get a chance to meet the other priests from the various centers as well as other students from across the country. People get a chance to see that the training is consistent across the country, as each priest carries a certain presence and light that is the signature of this priesthood.

There is a stamp of integrity and clear energy in the priests while each person is a unique soul that is distinct. We are not trying to make everyone the same. God inside each person and their soul makes them unique; we simply train people to become who they are as a soul. Likes and dislikes, opinions and concepts have to be rejected as these do not have much to do with the uniqueness of a human soul. All souls are alike in their ability to love and carry light, and these qualities are the ones we foster and develop in those souls we train.

———————

In the years following the expansion to four centers instead of two, we made many changes in how we function as a body of mystics. After a short introduction to our teachings, students can come regularly to our Tuesday night Bible Contemplation and Thursday night Tree of Life class. They are welcome, as well, to join us for daily meditation and Communion each morning. We have a regular Sunday meditation and Communion Service open to all, beginning at 9:30 a.m.

We have a consistent pattern and schedule at each of the centers so that if anyone is traveling, they will know to expect the same classes and services, no matter what city they are visiting. Evening prayers are also open to those who choose to join us. All of our priests serve the Sacraments, counsel with people, and teach classes.

Some people desire more consistent and intense training and can request to be a student. This involves closer work with the priest where they do meditations and spiritual exercises designed to bring them real experience of God and the light. Students who choose to live in close proximity to a priest might be invited to live in one of our centers. This is an immersion in the spiritual life and gives you a chance to get weekly training and deeper connection to the priest.

Training for the ministry involves becoming a deacon-in-training and working more directly with a priest. The role of deacons-in-training and deacons are often stepping stones, progressing towards the priesthood. Each has differing responsibilities and duties and works with a teacher. Deacons have to be illumined in order to be ordained and priests have to be Self-Realized.

Our ordinations are not based on an academic curriculum, as that would be ridiculous from our point of view. Academic training has not changed the world even a little. We are all mostly educated members of society, but academic studies are not the criterion upon which advancement or empowerment is based. Our empowerment is purely and simply based on whether the person has attained a certain degree of spiritual consciousness and responsiveness to God, Jesus, and Mary.

We might be interesting as a mystical order for those who are serious about their spiritual life and want to have an experience of God within them. To see God within, you have to have light, to be able to see the light within you when you close your eyes in a darkened room. This light is the light of Christ, that which will cause all the darkness to flee.

You will learn as the ancient sages learned, from experience and not from conjecture. Then, you will be able to join us in helping others to become one with God and to truly find peace.

For those people who are not near any of our centers, we offered online classes and training. We are serious about our spiritual mission and our work for the planet. The priesthood has virtually lost most of its integrity in the last few hundred years, and we are dedicated to bringing back the nobility, purity and integrity of the priesthood that Jesus and Mary represented when they were here. We are directly under their guidance, and we obey their commands. We are not under any denomination or religious tradition for a number of reasons. We have women priests as well as men, all of whom have dedicated their lives in service and in teaching for the raising up of people into sons and daughters of God. We represent a conscious, awake relationship with God at the center of our beings, because the Dominion of God is within.

Postscript

In spring of 2012, Mother Clare began to veer off in a different direction than was set out in the beginning of the Order, so we parted ways. I could not support changing the direction I was given by Jesus and Mary in how to teach and what to teach, so I started Ruach Center (Ruach means "Holy Spirit") with the more experienced priests. Things change and you move on.

I have to do what I am told from within.

About the Author

Father Peter Bowes is a Priest and Master Teacher in the mystical Christian order called Ruach Center. He has been teaching and training people on the inner spiritual path for many years. In addition, he has worked as a marriage and family therapist with Jungian training and has taught and trained therapists at the graduate level. Father Peter is a singer/songwriter/and writer.

His books are on Amazon and his music can be found on www.CDbaby.com and www.itunes.com .

Check out www.Ruachcenter.org.